LITTLE BO-PEEP

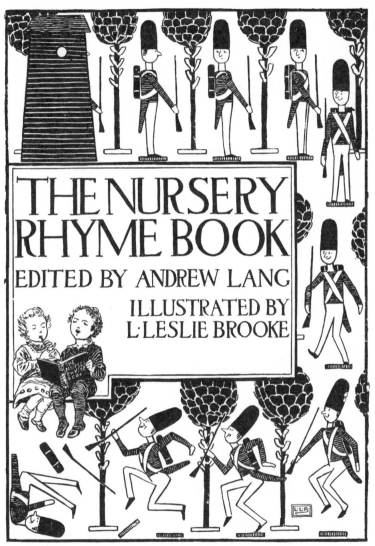

THE NURSERY RHYME BOOK

EDITED BY ANDREW LANG

ILLUSTRATED BY L·LESLIE BROOKE

DERRYDALE BOOKS · NEW YORK

This 1985 edition published by Derrydale Books,
distributed by Crown Publishers, Inc.

Library of Congress Cataloging in Publication Data

Main entry under title:

The Nursery rhyme book.

Reprint. Originally published: London, New York:
F. Warne, 1898.

Summary: A collection of 332 nursery rhymes grouped
under such categories as "Historical," "Tales," "Proverbs,"
"Songs," "Games," and "Jingles."

1. Nursery rhymes. 2. Children's poetry. [1. Nursery rhymes]
I. Lang, Andrew, 1844-1912. II. Brooke, L. Leslie
(Leonard Leslie), 1862-1940, ill.
PZ8.3.N933 1985 398'.8 85-4491
ISBN 0-517-47978-8

Manufactured in Yugoslavia.

Preface

TO read the old Nursery Rhymes brings back queer lost memories of a man's own childhood.   One seems to see the loose floppy picture-books of long ago, with their boldly coloured pictures.   The books were tattered and worn, and my first library consisted of a wooden box full of these volumes.   And I can remember being imprisoned for some crime in the closet where the box was, and how my gaolers found me, happy and impenitent, sitting on the box, with its contents all round me, reading.

There was "Who Killed Cock Robin?" which I knew by heart before I could read, and I learned to read (entirely "without tears") by picking out the letters in the familiar words. I remember the Lark dressed as a clerk, but what a clerk might be I did not ask. Other children, who are little now, will read this book, and remember it well when they have forgotten a great deal of history and geography. We do not know what poets wrote the old Nursery Rhymes, but certainly some of them were written down, or even printed, three hundred years ago. Grandmothers have sung them to their grandchildren, and they again to theirs, for many centuries. In Scotland an old fellow will take a child on his knee for a ride, and sing—

"This is the way the ladies ride,
Jimp and sma',—"

a smooth ride, then a rough trot,—

"This is the way the cadgers ride,
Creels and a'!"

Such songs are sometimes not printed, but they are never forgotten.

About the people mentioned in this book :—We do not exactly know who Old King Cole was, but King Arthur must have reigned some time about 500 to 600 A.D. As a child grows up, he will, if he is fond of poetry, read thousands of lines about this Prince, and the Table Round where his Knights dined, and how four weeping Queens carried him from his last fight to Avalon, a country where the apple-trees are always in bloom. But the reader will never forget the bag-pudding, which "the Queen next morning fried." Her name was Guinevere, and the historian says that she "was a true lover, and therefore made she a good end." But she had a great deal of unhappiness in her life.

I cannot tell what King of France went up the hill with twenty thousand men, and did nothing when he got there. But I do know who Charley was that "loved good ale and wine," and also "loved good brandy," and was fond of a pretty girl, "as sweet as sugar-candy." This was the banished Prince of Wales, who tried to win back his father's kingdom more than a hundred years ago, and gained battles, and took cities, and would have recovered the throne if his officers had followed him. But he was as unfortunate as he was brave, and when he had no longer a chance, perhaps he *did* love good ale and wine rather too dearly. As for the pretty girls, they all ran after him, and he could not run away like Georgey Porgey. There is plenty of poetry about Charley, as well as about King Arthur.

About King Charles the First, "upon a black horse," a child will soon hear at least as much as he can want, and perhaps his heart "will be ready to burst," as the rhyme says, with sorrow for the unhappy King. After he had his head cut off, "the Parliament soldiers went to the King," that is, to his son Charles, and crowned him in his turn, but he was thought a little too gay. Then we come to the King "who had a daughter fair, and gave the Prince of Orange her."

There is another rhyme about him :—

> " O what's the rhyme to porringer ?
> Ken ye the rhyme to porringer ?
> King James the Seventh had ae dochter,
> And he gave her to an Oranger.
>
> Ken ye how he requited him ?
> Ken ye how he requited him ?
> The lad has into England come,
> And ta'en the crown in spite o' him.
>
> The dog, he shall na keep it lang,
> To flinch we'll make him fain again ;
> We'll hing him hie upon a tree,
> And James shall have his ain again."

The truth is, that the Prince of Orange and the King's daughter fair (really a very pretty lady, with a very ugly husband) were not at all kind to the King, but turned him out of England. He was the grandfather of Charley who loved good ale and wine, and who very nearly turned out King Georgey Porgey, a German who " kissed the girls and made them cry," as the poet likewise says. Georgey was not a handsome King, and nobody cared much for him ; and if any poetry was made about him, it was

very bad stuff, and all the world has forgotten it.
He had a son called Fred, who was killed by a
cricket-ball—an honourable death.   A poem was
made when Fred died :—

> " Here lies Fred,
> Who was alive and is dead.
> If it had been his father,
> I would much rather ;
> If it had been his brother,
> Still better than another ;
> If it had been his sister,
> No one would have missed
>   her ;
> If it had been the whole gene-
>   ration,
> So much the better for the
>   nation.
> But as it's only Fred,
> Who was alive and is dead,
> Why there's no more to be
>   said."

This poet seems to have preferred Charley, who
wore a white rose in his bonnet, and was much
handsomer than Fred.

Another rhyme tells about Jim and George, and
how Jim got George by the nose.   This Jim was

Charley's father, and the George whom he "got by the nose" was Georgey Porgey, the fat German. Jim was born on June 10; so another song says—

> "Of all the days that's in the year,
>   The Tenth of June to me's most dear,
>   When our White Roses will appear
>   To welcome Jamie the Rover."

But, somehow, George really got Jim by the nose, in spite of what the poet says; for it does not do to believe all the history in song-books.

After these songs there is not much really useful information in the Nursery Rhymes. Simple Simon was not Simon Fraser of Lovat, who was sometimes on Jim's side, and sometimes on George's, till he got his head cut off by King George. That Simon was not simple.

The Babes in the Wood you may read about here and in longer poems; for instance, in a book called "The Ingoldsby Legends." It was their wicked uncle who lost them in the wood, because he wanted their money. Uncles were exceedingly bad long ago, and often smothered their nephews in the

Tower, or put out their eyes with red-hot irons.
But now uncles are the kindest people in the world,
as every child knows.

About Brian O'Lin there is more than this book
says :—

> " Brian O'Lin had no breeches to wear;
> He bought him a sheepskin to make him a pair,
> The woolly side out, and the other side in :
> ' It's pleasant and cool,' says Brian O'Lin."

He is also called Tom o' the Lin, and seems to
have been connected with Young Tamlane, who
was carried away by the Fairy Queen, and brought
back to earth by his true love.   Little Jack Horner
lived at a place called Mells, in Somerset, in the
time of Henry VIII.   The plum he got was an
estate which had belonged to the priests.   I find
nobody else here about whom history teaches us till
we come to Dr. Faustus.   He was *not* "a very
good man"; that is a mistake, or the poem was
written by a friend of the Doctor's.   In reality he
was a wizard, and raised up Helen of Troy from
the other world, the most beautiful woman who

ever was seen. Dr. Faustus made an agreement with Bogie, who, after the Doctor had been gay for a long time, came and carried him off in a flash of fire. You can read about it all in several books, when you are a good deal older. Dr. Faustus was a German, and the best play about him is by a German poet.

As to Tom the Piper's Son, he was probably the son of a Highlander, for they were mostly on Charley's side, who was "Over the hills and far away." Another song says—

> "There was a wind, it came to me
> Over the south and over the sea,
> And it has blown my corn and hay
> Over the hills and far away.
> But though it left me bare indeed,
> And blew my bonnet off my head,
> There's something hid in Highland brae,
> It has not blown my sword away.
> Then o'er the hills and over the dales,
> Over all England, and thro' Wales,
> The broadsword yet shall bear the sway,
> Over the hills and far away!"

Tom piped this tune, and pleased both the girls and boys.

About the two birds that sat on a stone, on the
" All-Alone Stone," you can read in a book called
" The Water-Babies."

Concerning the Frog that lived in a well, and how
he married a King's daughter and was changed into
a beautiful Prince, there is a fairy tale which an
industrious child ought to read. The frog in the
rhyme is not nearly so lucky.

After these rhymes there come a number of
riddles, of which the answers are given. Then
there are charms, which people used to think would
help in butter-making or would cure diseases. It
is not generally thought now that they are of much
use, but there can be no harm in trying. Nobody will be burned now for saying these charms,
like the poor old witches long ago. The Queen
Anne mentioned on page 172 was the sister of the
other Princess who married the Prince of Orange,
and she was Charley's aunt. She had seventeen
children, and only one lived to be as old as ten
years. He was a nice boy, and had a regiment of
boy-soldiers.

"Hickory Dickory Dock" is a rhyme for counting out a lot of children. The child on whom the last word falls has to run after the others in the game of "Tig" or "Chevy." There is another of the same kind :—

> " Onery
> Twoery
> Tickery
> Tin
> Alamacrack
> Tenamalin
> Pin
> Pan
> Musky Dan
> Tweedleum
> Twiddleum
> Twenty-one
> Black fish
> White trout
> Eery, Ory
> You are out."

Most of the rhymes in this part of the book are sung in games and dances by children, and are very pretty to see and hear. They are very old, too, and in an old book of travels in England by a Danish gentleman, he gives one which he heard sung by children when Charles II. was king. They still sing it in the North of Scotland.

In this collection there are nonsense songs to sing to babies to make them fall asleep.

Bessy Bell and Mary Gray, on page 207, were two young ladies in Scotland long ago. The plague came to Perth, where they lived, so they built a bower in a wood, far off the town. But their lovers came to see them in the bower, and brought the infection of the plague, and they both died. There is a little churchyard and a ruined church in Scotland, where the people who died of the plague, more than two hundred years ago, were buried, and we used to believe that if the ground was stirred, the plague would fly out again, like a yellow cloud, and kill everybody.

There is a French rhyme like " Blue - Eye Beauty "—

> " *Les yeux bleus*
> *Vont aux cieux.*
> *Les yeux gris*
> *Vont à Paradis.*
> *Les yeux noirs*
> *Vont à Purgatoire.*"

None of the other rhymes seem to be anything
but nonsense, and nonsense is a very good thing in
its way, especially with pictures.   Any child who
likes can get Mrs. Markham's "History of England,"
and read about the Jims, and Georges, and Charleys,
but I scarcely think that such children are very
common.   However, the facts about these famous
people are told here shortly, and if there is any
more to be said about Jack and Jill, I am sure I
don't know what it is, or where the hill they sat
on is to be found in the geography books.

Contents

Contents

Illustrations

Illustrations

D

The Nursery
Rhyme Book
•
I · Historical

OLD King Cole
    Was a merry old soul,
And a merry old soul was he;
He called for his pipe,
And he called for his bowl,
And he called for his fiddlers three.

Every fiddler, he had a fiddle,
And a very fine fiddle had he;
Twee tweedle dee, tweedle dee, went the fiddlers.
Oh, there's none so rare,
As can compare
With King Cole and his fiddlers three!

WHEN good King Arthur ruled this land,
    He was a goodly king;
He stole three pecks of barley-meal,
    To make a bag-pudding.

A bag-pudding the king did make,
    And stuff'd it well with plums:
And in it put great lumps of fat,
    As big as my two thumbs.

The king and queen did eat thereof,
    And noblemen beside;
And what they could not eat that night,
    The queen next morning fried.

HE STOLE THREE PECKS OF BARLEY-MEAL

E

I HAD a little nut-tree, nothing would it bear
  But a silver nutmeg and a golden pear;
The King of Spain's daughter came to visit me,
And all was because of my little nut-tree.
I skipp'd over water, I danced over sea,
And all the birds in the air couldn't catch me.

THE King of France, and four thousand men,
  They drew their swords, and put them up again.

THE King of France went up the hill,
  With twenty thousand men;
The King of France came down the hill,
  And ne'er went up again.

PLEASE to remember
  The Fifth of November,
Gunpowder treason and plot;
I know no reason
Why gunpowder treason
  Should ever be forgot.

O VER the water, and over the sea,
   And over the water to Charley;
Charley loves good ale and wine,
And Charley loves good brandy,
And Charley loves a pretty girl,
As sweet as sugar-candy.

Over the water, and over the sea,
And over the water to Charley;
I'll have none of your nasty beef,
Nor I'll have none of your barley;
But I'll have some of your very best flour,
To make a white cake for my Charley.

AS I was going by Charing Cross,
 I saw a black man upon a black horse ;
They told me it was King Charles the First ;
Oh, dear ! my heart was ready to burst !

HIGH diddle ding,
 Did you hear the bells ring ?
The parliament soldiers are gone to the King !
Some they did laugh, some they did cry,
To see the parliament soldiers pass by. ·

HECTOR PROTECTOR was dressed all in
 green ;
Hector Protector was sent to the Queen.
The Queen did not like him,
Nor more did the King ;
So Hector Protector was sent back again.

WHAT is the rhyme for *poringer* ?
 The King he had a daughter fair,
And gave the Prince of Orange her.

AS I walked by myself,
    And talked to myself,
  Myself said unto me,
Look to thyself,
Take care of thyself,
    For nobody cares for thee.

I answered myself,
And said to myself,
    In the self-same repartee,
Look to thyself,
Or not look to thyself,
    The self-same thing will be.

POOR old Robinson Crusoe!
    Poor old Robinson Crusoe!
They made him a coat
Of an old nanny goat,

    I wonder how they could do so!
With a ring a ting tang,
And a ring a ting tang,
    Poor old Robinson Crusoe!

THERE was a monkey climbed up a tree,
When he fell down, then down fell he.

There was a crow sat on a stone,
When he was gone, then there was none.

There was an old wife did eat an apple,
When she had eat two, she had eat a couple.

There was a horse going to the mill,
When he went on, he stood not still.

There was a butcher cut his thumb,
When it did bleed, then blood did come.

There was a lackey ran a race,
When he ran fast, he ran apace.

There was a cobbler clouting shoon,
When they were mended, they were done.

There was a chandler making candle,
When he them strip, he did them handle.

There was a navy went into Spain,
When it returned, it came again.

JIM and George were two great lords,
　They fought all in a churn;
And when that Jim got George by the nose,
　Then George began to girn.

SEE saw, sack-a-day;
　Monmouth is a pretie boy,
　Richmond is another,
Grafton is my onely joy;
And why should I these three destroy,
　To please a pious brother![1]

---

[1] The boys are sons of Charles II.　The pious brother is
James, Duke of York.

LITERAL &
SCHOLASTIC

F

GREAT A, little a,
   Bouncing B!
The cat's in the cupboard,
And can't see me.

43

IF ifs and ands,
Were pots and pans,
There would be no need for tinkers!

TELL tale, tit!
Your tongue shall be slit,
And all the dogs in the town
Shall have a little bit.

BIRCH and green holly, boys,
Birch and green holly.
If you get beaten, boys,
'Twill be your own folly.

COME when you're called,
Do what you're bid,
Shut the door after you,
Never be chid.

WAS an Archer,
  and shot at a frog,
B was a Butcher,
  and had a great dog.
C was a Captain,
  all covered with lace,
D was a Drunkard,
  and had a red face.
   E was an Esquire,
    with pride on his
    brow,
F was a Farmer, and followed the plough.
G was a Gamester, who had but ill luck,
H was a Hunter, and hunted a buck.
I was an Innkeeper, who loved to bouse,
J was a Joiner, and built up a house.
K was King William, once governed this land,
L was a Lady, who had a white hand.
M was a Miser, and hoarded up gold,
N was a Nobleman, gallant and bold.
O was an Oyster Wench, and went about town,
P was a Parson, and wore a black gown.
Q was a Queen, who was fond of good flip,
R was a Robber, and wanted a whip.
S was a Sailor, and spent all he got,

T was a Tinker, and mended a pot.
U was an Usurer, a miserable elf,
V was a Vintner, who drank all himself.
W was a Watchman, and guarded the door,
X was expensive, and so became poor.
Y was a Youth, that did not love school,
Z was a Zany, a poor harmless fool.

A WAS an apple-pie;
  B bit it;
C cut it;
D dealt it;
E ate it;
F fought for it;
G got it;
H had it;
J joined it;
K kept it;
L longed for it;
M mourned for it;
N nodded at it;
O opened it;

P peeped in it;
Q quartered it;
R ran for it;
S stole it;
T took it;
V viewed it,
W wanted it;
X, Y, Z, and amperse-and,
All wish'd for a piece in hand.

PAT-A-CAKE, pat-a-cake, baker's man!
(So I will, master), as fast as I can:
Pat it, and prick it, and mark it with T,
Put in the oven for Tommy and me.

MULTIPLICATION is vexation,
Division is as bad;
The Rule of Three doth puzzle me,
And Practice drives me mad.

DOCTOR FAUSTUS was a good man,
He whipt his scholars now and then;
When he whipp'd them he made them dance,
Out of Scotland into France,
Out of France into Spain,
And then he whipp'd them back again!

A DILLER, a dollar,
    A ten o'clock scholar,
What makes you come so soon?
You used to come at ten o'clock,
But now you come at noon.

WHEN V and I together meet,
    They make the number Six compleat.
When I with V doth meet once more,
Then 'tis they Two can make but Four.
And when that V from I is gone,
Alas! poor I can make but One.

THIRTY days hath September,
    April, June, and November;
February has twenty-eight alone,
All the rest have thirty-one,
Excepting leap-year, that's the time
When February's days are twenty-nine.

G

MISTRESS MARY, quite contrary,
    How does your garden grow?
With cockle-shells, and silver bells,
    And pretty maids all a row.

IN fir tar is,
  In oak none is.
In mud eel is,
In clay none is.
Goat eat ivy,
Mare eat oats.

CROSS patch,
  Draw the latch,
Sit by the fire and spin ;
  Take a cup,
  And drink it up,
Then call your neighbours in.

I LOVE my love with an A, because he's Agreeable.
  I hate him because he's Avaricious.
He took me to the Sign of the Acorn,
And treated me with Apples.
His name's Andrew,
And he lives at Arlington.

ONE, two,
     Buckle my shoe;
Three, four,
Shut the door;
Five, six,
Pick up sticks;
Seven, eight,
Lay them straight;
Nine, ten,
A good fat hen;

Eleven, twelve,
Who will delve?
Thirteen, fourteen,
Maids a-courting;
Fifteen, sixteen,
Maids a-kissing;
Seventeen, eighteen,
Maid a-waiting;
Nineteen, twenty,
My stomach's empty.

TALES

THE man in the moon,
Came tumbling down,
And ask'd his way to Norwich,
He went by the south,
And burnt his mouth
With supping cold pease-porridge.

M Y dear, do you know,
How a long time ago,
Two poor little children,
Whose names I don't know,
Were stolen away on a fine summer's day,
And left in a wood, as I've heard people say.

And when it was night,
So sad was their plight,
The sun it went down,
And the moon gave no light.
They sobbed and they sighed, and they bitterly
cried,
And the poor little things, they lay down and died.

And when they were dead,
The Robins so red
Brought strawberry-leaves
And over them spread;
And all the day long
They sung them this song:
"Poor babes in the wood!   Poor babes in the wood!
And don't you remember the babes in the wood?"

THERE was a crooked man, and he went a
crooked mile,
He found a crooked sixpence against a crooked stile:
He bought a crooked cat, which caught a crooked
mouse,
And they all lived together in a little crooked house.

S IMPLE SIMON met a pieman,
  Going to the fair ;
Says Simple Simon to the pieman,
  " Let me taste your ware."

Says the pieman to Simple Simon,
  " Show me first your penny."
Says Simple Simon to the pieman,
  " Indeed I have not any."

Simple Simon went a-fishing
  For to catch a whale :
All the water he had got
  Was in his mother's pail !

I 'LL tell you a story
  About Jack a Nory,—
And now my story's begun :
  I'll tell you another
  About Jack his brother,—
And now my story's done.

SIMPLE SIMON

THERE was a man, and he had nought,
　　And robbers came to rob him;
He crept up to the chimney-pot,
　　And then they thought they had him.

But he got down on t' other side,
　　And then they could not find him.
He ran fourteen miles in fifteen days,
　　And never looked behind him.

T HE lion and the unicorn
    Were fighting for the crown;
The lion beat the unicorn
    All round about the town.

Some gave them white bread,
 And some gave them brown;
Some gave them plum-cake,
 And sent them out of town.

THERE was a fat man of Bombay,
 Who was smoking one sunshiny day,
When a bird, called a snipe,
Flew away with his pipe,
Which vexed the fat man of Bombay.

TOM, Tom, the piper's son,
 Stole a pig, and away he run!
The pig was eat, and Tom was beat,
And Tom went roaring down the street.

BRYAN O'LIN, and his wife, and wife's mother,
 They all went over a bridge together;
The bridge was broken, and they all fell in,
The deuce go with all! quoth Bryan O'Lin.

THERE was a little man,
And he had a little gun,
And his bullets were made of

lead,

lead,

lead ;

He went to the brook
And saw a little duck,
And he shot it right through the head, head, head.

He carried it home
To his old wife Joan,
And bid her a fire for to make, make, make ;
To roast the little duck
He had shot in the brook,
And he'd go and fetch her the drake, drake, drake.

THREE wise men of Gotham
  Went to sea in a bowl:
And if the bowl had been stronger,
My song would have been longer.

DOCTOR FOSTER went to Glo'ster
  In a shower of rain;
He stepped in a puddle, up to his middle,
  And never went there again.

ROBIN the Bobbin, the big-bellied Ben,
   He ate more meat than fourscore men ;
He ate a cow, he ate a calf,
He ate a butcher and a half ;
He ate a church, he ate a steeple,
He ate the priest and all the people !
      A cow and a calf,
      An ox and a half,
      A church and a steeple,
      And all the good people,
And yet he complained that his stomach wasn't full.

ROBIN and Richard were two pretty men ;
   They laid in bed till the clock struck ten ;
Then up starts Robin and looks at the sky,
Oh ! brother Richard, the sun's very high :

The bull's in the barn threshing the corn,
The cock's on the dunghill blowing his horn,
The cat's at the fire frying of fish,
The dog's in the pantry breaking his dish.

OLD Mother Goose, when
    She wanted to wander,
Would ride through the air
On a very fine gander.

Mother Goose had a house,
'Twas built in a wood,
Where an owl at the door
For sentinel stood.

This is her son Jack,
A plain-looking lad,.
He is not very good,
Nor yet very bad.

She sent him to market,
A live goose he bought,
Here, mother, says he,
It will not go for nought.

Jack's goose and her gander
Grew very fond ;
They'd both eat together,
Or swim in one pond.

Jack found one morning,
As I have been told,
His goose had laid him
An egg of pure gold.

Jack rode to his mother
The news for to tell;
She call'd him a good boy,
And said it was well.

Jack sold his gold egg
To a rogue of a Jew
Who cheated him out of
The half of his due.

Then Jack went a-courting
A lady so gay,
As fair as the lily,
And sweet as the May.

The Jew and the Squire
Came behind his back,
And began to belabour
The sides of poor Jack.

The old Mother Goose
That instant came in,
And turned her son Jack
Into famed Harlequin.

She then with her wand
Touch'd the lady so fine,
And turn'd her at once
Into sweet Columbine.

The gold egg into the sea
Was thrown then,—
When Jack jump'd in,
And got the egg back again.

The Jew got the goose,
Which he vow'd he would kill,
Resolving at once
His pockets to fill.

Jack's mother came in,
And caught the goose soon,
And mounting its back,
Flew up to the moon.

OLD Abram Brown is dead and gone,
You'll never see him more;
He used to wear a long brown coat,
That button'd down before.

MY lady Wind, my lady Wind,
   Went round about the house to find
   A chink to get her foot in :
She tried the key-hole in the door,
She tried the crevice in the floor,
   And drove the chimney soot in.

And then one night when it was dark,
She blew up such a tiny spark,
   That all the house was pothered :
From it she raised up such a flame,
As flamed away to Belting Lane,
   And White Cross folks were smothered.

And thus when once, my little dears,
A whisper reaches itching ears,
   The same will come, you'll find :
Take my advice, restrain the tongue,
Remember what old nurse has sung
   Of busy lady Wind.

PUNCH and Judy
   Fought for a pie ;
Punch gave Judy
   A sad blow on the eye.

TAFFY was a Welshman, Taffy was a thief;
   Taffy came to my house and stole a piece
      of beef:
I went to Taffy's house, Taffy was not at home;
Taffy came to my house and stole a marrow-
      bone.

I went to Taffy's house, Taffy was not in;
Taffy came to my house and stole a silver pin:
I went to Taffy's house, Taffy was in bed,
I took up a poker and flung it at his head.

LITTLE Tommy Tittlemouse
Lived in a little house;
He caught fishes
In other men's ditches.

K

LITTLE Jack Horner sat in a corner,
   Eating a Christmas pie ;
He put in his thumb, and he pulled out a plum,
   And said, " What a good boy am I ! "

SOLOMON GRUNDY,
   Born on a Monday,
Christened on Tuesday,
Married on Wednesday,
Took ill on Thursday,
Worse on Friday,
Died on Saturday,
Buried on Sunday :
This is the end
Of Solomon Grundy.

PROVERBS

TO make your candles last for a',
   You wives and maids give ear-o!
To put 'em out's the only way,
   Says honest John Boldero.

ST. SWITHIN'S day, if thou dost rain,
  For forty days it will remain :
St. Swithin's day, if thou be fair,
  For forty days 'twill rain na mair.

IF wishes were horses,
  Beggars would ride ;
If turnips were watches,
  I would wear one by my side.

NATURE requires five,
  Custom gives seven !
Laziness takes nine,
  And Wickedness eleven.   [*Hours of Sleep.*

SEE a pin and pick it up,
  All the day you'll have good luck ;
See a pin and let it lay,
Bad luck you'll have all the day !

NEEDLES and pins, needles and pins,
When a man marries his trouble begins.

BOUNCE BUCKRAM, velvet's dear;
Christmas comes but once a year.

A MAN of words and not of deeds,
Is like a garden full of weeds;
And when the weeds begin to grow,
It's like a garden full of snow;
And when the snow begins to fall,
It's like a bird upon the wall;
And when the bird away does fly,
It's like an eagle in the sky;
And when the sky begins to roar,
It's like a lion at the door;
And when the door begins to crack,
It's like a stick across your back;
And when your back begins to smart,
It's like a penknife in your heart;
And when your heart begins to bleed,
You're dead, and dead, and dead, indeed.

IF you sneeze on Monday, you sneeze for danger;
Sneeze on a Tuesday, kiss a stranger;
Sneeze on a Wednesday, sneeze for a letter;
Sneeze on a Thursday, something better;
Sneeze on a Friday, sneeze for sorrow;
Sneeze on a Saturday, see your sweetheart to-morrow.

WHEN the wind is in the east,
'Tis neither good for man nor beast;
When the wind is in the north,
The skilful fisher goes not forth;

When the wind is in the south,
It blows the bait in the fishes' mouth;

When the wind is in the west,
Then 'tis at the very best.

HE that would thrive
   Must rise at five;
He that hath thriven
May lie till seven;
And he that by the plough would thrive,
Himself must either hold or drive.

L

A SWARM of bees in May
  Is worth a load of hay;
A swarm of bees in June
Is worth a silver spoon;
A swarm of bees in July
Is not worth a fly.

YEOW mussent sing a' Sunday,
  Becaze it is a sin,
But yeow may sing a' Monday
Till Sunday cums agin.

A SUNSHINY shower
  Won't last half an hour.

FOR every evil under the sun,
  There is a remedy, or there is none.
If there be one, try and find it;
If there be none, never mind it.

THE art of good driving s a paradox quite,
　　Though custom has prov'd it so long;
If you go to the left, you're sure to go right,
　　If you go to the right, you go wrong.

※

AS the days lengthen,
　　So the storms strengthen.

※

THE fair maid who, the first of May,
　　Goes to the fields at break of day,
And washes in dew from the hawthorn tree,
Will ever after handsome be.

※

FRIDAY night's dream,
　　On the Saturday told,
　　Is sure to come true,
　　　　Be it never so old.

※

EARLY to bed, and early to rise,
　　Makes a man healthy, wealthy, and wise.

MONDAY'S bairn is fair of face,
Tuesday's bairn is full of grace,
Wednesday's bairn is full of woe,
Thursday's bairn has far to go,
Friday's bairn is loving and giving,
Saturday's bairn works hard for its living,
But the bairn that is born on the Sabbath day
Is bonny and blithe, and good and gay.

FOR want of a nail, the shoe was lost;
For want of the shoe, the horse was lost;
For want of the horse, the rider was lost;
For want of the rider, the battle was lost;
For want of the battle, the kingdom was lost;
And all from the want of a horseshoe nail.

MARCH winds and April showers
Bring forth May flowers.

SONGS

ONE misty moisty morning,
    When cloudy was the weather,
There I met an old man
Clothed all in leather;

Clothed all in leather,
With cap under his chin,—
How do you do, and how do you do,
And how do you do again!

THE fox and his wife they had a great strife,
    They never eat mustard in all their whole life;
They eat their meat without fork or knife,
    And loved to be picking a bone, e-ho!

The fox jumped up on a moonlight night;
The stars they were shining, and all things bright;
Oh, ho! said the fox, it's a very fine night
    For me to go through the town, e-ho!

The fox when he came to yonder stile,
He lifted his lugs and he listened a while!
Oh, ho! said the fox, it's but a short mile
    From this unto yonder wee town, e-ho!

The fox when he came to the farmer's gate,
Who should he see but the farmer's drake;
I love you well for your master's sake,
    And long to be picking your bone, e-ho!

The grey goose she ran round the hay-stack,
Oh, ho! said the fox, you are very fat;
You'll grease my beard and ride on my back
From this into yonder wee town, e-ho!

Old Gammer Hipple-hopple hopped out of bed,
She opened the casement, and popped out her head;
Oh! husband, oh! husband, the grey goose is dead,
And the fox is gone through the town, oh!

Then the old man got up in his red cap,
And swore he would catch the fox in a trap;
But the fox was too cunning, and gave him the slip,
And ran through the town, the town, oh!

When he got up to the top of the hill,
He blew his trumpet both loud and shrill,
For joy that he was safe
Through the town, oh!

When the fox came back to his den,
He had young ones both nine and ten,
" You're welcome home, daddy, you may go again,
If you bring us such nice meat
From the town, oh!"

M

MY father he died, but I can't tell you how;
He left me six horses to drive in my plough:
  With my wing wang waddle oh,
  Jack sing saddle oh,
  Blowsey boys buble oh,
  Under the broom.

I sold my six horses and I bought me a cow,
I'd fain have made a fortune but did not know
    how:
  With my, &c.

I sold my cow, and I bought me a calf;
I'd fain have made a fortune, but lost the best
    half!
  With my, &c.

I sold my calf, and I bought me a cat;
A pretty thing she was, in my chimney corner sat:
  With my, &c.

I sold my cat, and bought me a mouse;
He carried fire in his tail, and burnt down my
    house:
  With my, &c.

SAYS t'auld man tit oak tree,
  Young and lusty was I when I kenn'd thee;
I was young and lusty, I was fair and clear,
Young and lusty was I mony a lang year;
But sair fail'd am I, sair fail'd now,
Sair fail'd am I sen I kenn'd thou.

POLLY put the kettle on,
    Polly put the kettle on,
Polly put the kettle on,
    And let's drink tea.

Sukey take it off again,
Sukey take it off again,
Sukey take it off again,
    They're all gone away

LITTLE BO-PEEP has lost her sheep,
    And can't tell where to find them;
Leave them alone, and they'll come home,
    And bring their tails behind them.

Little Bo-peep fell fast asleep,
    And dreamt she heard them bleating;
But when she awoke, she found it a joke,
    For they were still a-fleeting.

Then up she took her little crook,
    Determin'd for to find them;
She found them indeed, but it made her heart bleed,
    For they'd left all their tails behind 'em.

SING a song of sixpence,
    A bag full of rye;
Four and twenty blackbirds
    Baked in a pie;

When the pie was open'd,
    The birds began to sing;
Was not that a dainty dish,
    To set before the king?

The king was in his counting-house
    Counting out his money;
The queen was in the parlour
    Eating bread and honey;

The maid was in the garden
    Hanging out the clothes,
There came a little blackbird,
    And snapt off her nose.

JOHNNY shall have a new bonnet,
    And Johnny shall go to the fair,
And Johnny shall have a blue ribbon
    To tie up his bonny brown hair.

And why may not I love Johnny?
　And why may not Johnny love me?
And why may not I love Johnny
　As well as another body?
And here's a leg for a stocking,
　And here is a leg for a shoe,
And he has a kiss for his daddy,
　And two for his mammy, I trow.
And why may not I love Johnny?
　And why may not Johnny love me?
And why may not I love Johnny,
　As well as another body?

ELSIE MARLEY is grown so fine,
　She won't get up to serve the swine,
But lies in bed till eight or nine,
And surely she does take her time.

And do you ken Elsie Marley, honey?
The wife who sells the barley, honey?
She won't get up to serve her swine,
And do you ken Elsie Marley, honey?

TOM he was a piper's son,
    He learn'd to play when he was young,
But all the tunes that he could play,
Was " Over the hills and far away ; "

Over the hills, and a great way off,
And the wind will blow my top-knot off.

Now Tom with his pipe made such a
        noise,
That he pleas'd both the girls and boys,
And they stopp'd to hear him play
" Over the hills and far away."

Tom with his pipe did play with such skill,
That those who heard him could never keep still;
Whenever they heard they began for to dance,
Even pigs on their hind legs would after him
    prance.

L. L. B.

As Dolly was milking her cow one day,
Tom took out his pipe and began for to play;
So Doll and the cow danced " the Cheshire round,"
Till the pail was broke, and the milk ran on the
    ground.

He met old Dame Trot with a basket of eggs;
He used his pipe, and she used her legs;
She danced about till the eggs were all broke;
She began for to fret, but he laughed at the joke.

He saw a cross fellow was beating an ass,
Heavy laden with pots, pans, dishes, and glass;
He took out his pipe and played them a tune,
And the jackass's load was lightened full soon.

N

LONDON BRIDGE is broken down,
    Dance o'er my Lady Lee;
London Bridge is broken down,
    With a gay lady.

How shall we build it up again?
    Dance o'er my Lady Lee;
How shall we build it up again?
    With a gay lady.

Build it up with silver and gold,
    Dance o'er my Lady Lee;
Build it up with silver and gold,
    With a gay lady.

Silver and gold will be stole away,
    Dance o'er my Lady Lee;
Silver and gold will be stole away,
    With a gay lady.

Build it up with iron and steel,
    Dance o'er my Lady Lee;
Build it up with iron and steel,
    With a gay lady.

Iron and steel will bend and bow,
　　Dance o'er my Lady Lee;
Iron and steel will bend and bow,
　　With a gay lady.

Build it up with wood and clay,
　　Dance o'er my Lady Lee;
Build it up with wood and clay,
　　With a gay lady.

Wood and clay will wash away,
　　Dance o'er my Lady Lee;
Wood and clay will wash away,
　　With a gay lady.

Build it up with stone so strong,
　　Dance o'er my Lady Lee;
Huzza! 'twill last for ages long,
　　With a gay lady.

I LOVE sixpence, pretty little sixpence,
　　I love sixpence better than my life;
I spent a penny of it, I spent another,
　　And took fourpence home to my wife.

Oh, my little fourpence, pretty little fourpence,
  I love fourpence better than my life;
I spent a penny of it, I spent another,
  And I took twopence home to my wife.

Oh, my little twopence, my pretty little twopence,
  I love twopence better than my life;
I spent a penny of it, I spent another,
  And I took nothing home to my wife.

Oh, my little nothing, my pretty little nothing,
  What will nothing buy for my wife?
I have nothing, I spend nothing,
  I love nothing better than my wife.

THE north wind doth blow,
  And we shall have snow,
And what will poor Robin do then?
        Poor thing!

He'll sit in a barn,
  And to keep himself warm,
Will hide his head under his wing.
        Poor thing!

HE'LL SIT IN A BARN.

A CARRION crow sat on an oak,
 Fol de riddle, lol de riddle, hi ding do,
Watching a tailor shape his cloak;
 Sing heigh ho, the carrion crow,
 Fol de riddle, lol de riddle, hi ding do.

Wife, bring me my old bent bow,
 Fol de riddle, lol de riddle, hi ding do,
That I may shoot yon carrion crow;
 Sing heigh ho, the carrion crow,
 Fol de riddle, lol de riddle, hi ding do.

The tailor he shot and missed his mark,
 Fol de riddle, lol de riddle, hi ding do,
And shot his own sow quite through the heart;
 Sing heigh ho, the carrion crow,
 Fol de riddle, lol de riddle, hi ding do.

Wife, bring brandy in a spoon,
 Fol de riddle, lol de riddle, hi ding do,
For our old sow is in a swoon;
 Sing heigh ho, the carrion crow,
 Fol de riddle, lol de riddle, hi ding do.

"Merry are the Bells & merry do they ring"

MERRY are the bells, and merry would they
ring;
Merry was myself, and merry could I sing;
With a merry ding-dong, happy, gay, and free,
And a merry sing-song, happy let us be!

Waddle goes your gait, and hollow are your hose;
Noddle goes your pate, and purple is your nose;
Merry is your sing-song, happy, gay, and free,
With a merry ding-dong, happy let us be!

Merry have we met, and merry have we been ;
Merry let us part, and merry meet again ;
With our merry sing-song, happy, gay, and free,
And a merry ding-dong, happy let us be !

HOT-CROSS Buns !
Hot-cross Buns !
One a penny, two a penny,
Hot-cross Buns !

Hot-cross Buns !
Hot-cross Buns !
If ye have no daughters,
Give them to your sons.

THREE blind mice, see how they run !
They all ran after the farmer's wife,
Who cut off their tails with the carving-knife ;
Did you ever see such fools in your life ?
Three blind mice.

YOU shall have an apple,
　　You shall have a plum,
You shall have a rattle-basket,
　　When your dad comes home.

THERE was a frog liv'd in a well,
　　Kitty alone, Kitty alone;
There was a frog liv'd in a well,
　　Kitty alone, and I!

There was a frog liv'd in a well,
　　And a farce[1] mouse in a mill;
　　Cock me cary, Kitty alone,
　　Kitty alone and I.

This frog he would a-wooing ride,
　　Kitty alone, &c.;
This frog he would a-wooing ride,
And on a snail he got astride,
　　Cock me cary, &c.

---

[1] Merry.

He rode till he
came to my
Lady Mouse
hall,

Kitty alone,
&c. ;

He rode till he
came to my
Lady Mouse
hall,

And there he
did both
knock and
call ;

Cock me cary,
&c.

Quoth he, " Miss Mouse, I'm come to thee,"
   Kitty alone, &c. ;
Quoth he, " Miss Mouse, I'm come to thee,
To see if thou canst fancy me ; "
   Cock me cary, &c.

Quoth she, " Answer I'll give you none,"
   Kitty alone, &c. ;
Quoth she, " Answer I'll give you none,
Until my uncle Rat come home ; "
   Cock me cary, &c.

And when her uncle Rat came home,
   Kitty alone, &c. ;
And when her uncle Rat came home,
" Who's been here since I've been gone ? "
   Cock me cary, &c.

" Sir, there's been a worthy gentleman,"
   Kitty alone, &c. ;
" Sir, there's been a worthy gentleman,
That's been here since you've been gone ; "
   Cock me cary, &c.

The frog he came whistling through the brook,
Kitty alone, &c.
The frog he came whistling through the brook,
And there he met with a dainty duck,
Cock me cary, &c.

This duck she swallow'd him up with a pluck,
Kitty alone, Kitty alone;
This duck she swallow'd him up with a pluck,
So there's an end of my history book.
Cock me cary, Kitty alone,
Kitty alone and I.

THERE were two birds sat on a stone,
    Fa, la, la, la, lal, de;
One flew away, and then there was one,
    Fa, la, la, la, lal, de;
The other flew after, and then there was none,
    Fa, la, la, la, lal, de;
And so the poor stone was left all alone,
    Fa, la, la, la, lal, de!

WHERE are you going, my pretty maid?"
    "I'm going a-milking, sir," she said.
"May I go with you, my pretty maid?"
"You're kindly welcome, sir," she said.
"What is your father, my pretty maid?"
"My father's a farmer, sir," she said.

"Say, will you marry me, my pretty maid?
"Yes, if you please, kind sir," she said.
"What is your fortune, my pretty maid?"
"My face is my fortune, sir," she said.
"Then I can't marry you, my pretty maid!"
"Nobody asked you, sir," she said.

THERE was a jolly miller
    Lived on the river Dee:
He worked and sung from morn till night,
    No lark so blithe as he;
And this the burden of his song
    For ever used to be—
I jump mejerrime jee!
    I care for nobody—no! not I,
Since nobody cares for me.

IF I'd as much money as I could spend,
    I never would cry old chairs to mend;
Old chairs to mend, old chairs to mend,
I never would cry old chairs to mend.

If I'd as much money as I could tell,
I never would cry old clothes to sell;
Old clothes to sell, old clothes to sell,
I never would cry old clothes to sell.

MY maid Mary
    She minds her dairy,
        While I go a-hoeing and mowing each morn.

Merrily run the reel
And the little spinning-wheel
    Whilst I am singing and mowing my corn.

✿

U P at Piccadilly oh !
    The coachman takes his stand,
And when he meets a pretty girl,
    He takes her by the hand.
        Whip away for ever oh !
        Drive away so clever oh !
        All the way to Bristol oh !
    He drives her four-in-hand.

✿

J ACKY, come give me thy fiddle,
    If ever thou mean to thrive : "
" Nay ; I'll not give my fiddle
    To any man alive.

" If I should give my fiddle,
    They'll think that I'm gone mad,
For many a joyful day
    My fiddle and I have had."

P

I 'LL sing you a song,
  Though not very long,
    Yet I think it as pretty as any.
Put your hand in your purse,
You'll never be worse,
    And give the poor singer a penny.

L ITTLE Polly Flinders
  Sat among the cinders,
Warming her pretty little toes.
Her mother came and caught her,
And whipped her little daughter
For spoiling her nice new clothes.

J OHN COOK had a little grey mare; he, haw,
  hum!
Her back stood up, and her bones they were bare;
    he, haw, hum!

John Cook was riding up Shuter's bank; he, haw,
    hum!
And there his nag did kick and prank; he, haw, hum!

John Cook was riding up Shuter's hill; he, haw,
  hum!
His mare fell down, and she made her will; he, haw,
  hum!

The bridle and saddle were laid on the shelf; he,
  haw, hum!
If you want any **more** you may sing it yourself; he,
  haw, hum!

RIDE away, ride away, Johnny shall ride,
  And he shall have pussy-cat tied to one side,
And he shall have little dog tied to the other,
And Johnny shall ride to see his grandmother.

THE Queen of Hearts,
  She made some tarts,
    All on a summer's day;
The Knave of Hearts,
He stole those tarts,
    And took them clean away.

The King of Hearts
Called for the tarts,
    And beat the Knave full sore;
The Knave of Hearts
Brought back the tarts,
    And vowed he'd steal no more.

THERE was a little woman, as I've been told,
  Who was not very young, nor yet very old;
Now this little woman her living got,
By selling codlins, hot, hot, hot.

DAME, get up and bake your pies,
  Bake your pies, bake your pies;
Dame, get up and bake your pies
On Christmas Day in the morning.

Dame, what makes your maidens lie,
Maidens lie, maidens lie;
Dame, what makes your maidens lie
On Christmas Day in the morning?

Dame, what makes your ducks to die,
Ducks to die, ducks to die;
Dame, what makes your ducks to die
On Christmas Day in the morning?

Their wings are cut and they cannot fly,
Cannot fly, cannot fly;
Their wings are cut and they cannot fly
On Christmas Day in the morning.

COLD and raw the north wind doth blow,
  Bleak in a morning early;
All the hills are covered with snow,
    And winter's now come fairly.

I SAW three ships come sailing by,
  Come sailing by, come sailing by;

I saw three ships come sailing by,
    On New Year's Day in the morning.

And what do you think was in them then,
    Was in them then, was in them then?
And what do you think was in them then,
    On New Year's Day in the morning?

Three pretty girls were in them then,
    Were in them then, were in them then;
Three pretty girls were in them then,
    On New Year's Day in the morning.

And one could whistle, and one could sing,
    And one could play on the violin—
Such joy there was at my wedding,
    On New Year's day in the morning.

WEE Willie Winkie runs through the town,
    Upstairs and downstairs in his nightgown,
Rapping at the window, crying through the lock,
"Are the children in their beds, for now it's eight
    o'clock?"

WHEN Little Fred was called to bed,
 He always acted right;
He kissed Mamma, and then Papa,
 And wished them all good night.

He made no noise, like naughty boys,
 But gently upstairs
Directly went, when he was sent,
 And always said his prayers.

RIDDLES & PARADOXES

I WENT to the wood and got it;
   I sat me down and looked at it;
The more I looked at it the less I liked it;
And I brought it home because I couldn't help it.

[A thorn.

HICK-A-MORE, Hack-a-more,
On the king's kitchen door;
All the king's horses,
And all the king's men,
Couldn't drive Hick-a-more, Hack-a-more,
Off the king's kitchen door!   [*Sunshine.*

AS soft as silk, as white as milk,
As bitter as gall, a thick wall,
And a green coat covers me all.
                    [*A walnut.*

LONG legs, crooked thighs,
Little head, and no eyes.
                    [*Pair of tongs.*

ARTHUR O'BOWER has broken his band,
He comes roaring up the land;—
The King of Scots, with all his power,
Cannot turn Arthur of the Bower!

                    [*A storm of wind.*

ARTHUR O'BOWER HAS BROKEN HIS BAND

THERE was a king met a king
  In a narrow lane;
Says this king to that king,
  "Where have you been?"

"Oh! I've been a hunting
  With my dog and my doe."
"Pray lend him to me,
  That I may do so."

"There's the dog *take* the dog."
  "What's the dog's name?"
"I've told you already."
  "Pray tell me again."

IN marble walls as white as milk,
  Lined with a skin as soft as silk;
Within a fountain crystal clear,
A golden apple doth appear.
No doors there are to this stronghold.
Yet things break in and steal the gold.

                    [*An egg.*

FLOUR of England, fruit of Spain,
Met together in a shower of rain ;
Put in a bag tied round with a string,
If you'll tell me this riddle, I'll give you a ring.

[*A plum-pudding.*

I HAVE a little sister, they call her Peep, Peep ;
She wades the waters deep, deep, deep ;
She climbs the mountains high, high, high ;
Poor little creature she has but one eye.

[*A star.*

HIGGLEDY piggledy
Here we lie,
Pick'd and pluck'd,
And put in a pie.
My first is snapping, snarling, growling,
My second's industrious, romping, and prowling.
Higgledy piggledy
Here we lie,
Pick'd and pluck'd,
And put in a pie.   [*Currants.*

H UMPTY DUMPTY sate on a wall;
  Humpty Dumpty had a great fall;
Three score men and three score more
Cannot place Humpty Dumpty as he was before.
                            [*An egg.*

T HIRTY white horses upon a red hill,
  Now they tramp, now they champ, now they
      stand still.   [*Teeth and gums.*

THOMAS A TATTAMUS took two T's,
    To tie two tups to two tall trees,
To frighten the terrible Thomas a Tattamus!
Tell me how many T's there are in all THAT.

OLD mother Twitchett had but one eye,
    And a long tail which she let fly;
And every time she went over a gap,
She left a bit of her tail in a trap.

[*A needle and thread.*

LITTLE Nancy Etticoat
    In a white petticoat,
And a red rose.
The longer she stands
The shorter she grows.   [*A candle.*

BLACK we are but much admired;
    Men seek for us till they are tired.
We tire the horse, but comfort man;
Tell me this riddle if you can.   [*Coals.*

THERE were three sisters in a hall ;
    There came a knight amongst them all :
Good morrow, aunt, to the one ;
Good morrow, aunt, to the other ;
Good morrow, gentlewoman, to the third ;
    If you were my aunt,
        As the other two be,
    I would say good morrow,
    Then, aunts, all three.

FORMED long ago, yet made to-day,
    Employed while others sleep ;
What few would like to give away,
    Nor any wish to keep.   [*A Bed.*

AS I was going to St. Ives,
    I met a man with seven wives ;
Every wife had seven sacks,
Every sack had seven cats,
Every cat had seven kits :
Kits, cats, sacks, and wives,
How many were there going to St. Ives ?

AS I went through the garden gap,
Who should I meet but Dick Red-cap!
A stick in his hand, a stone in his throat,
If you'll tell me this riddle, I'll give you a groat.

[*A cherry.*

AS I was going o'er Westminster bridge,
I met with a Westminster scholar;
He pulled off his cap, *an' drew* off his glove,
And wished me a very good morrow.
What is his name?

TWO legs sat upon three legs,
With one leg in his lap;
In comes four legs,
And runs away with one leg.
Up jumps two legs,
Catches up three legs,
Throws it after four legs,
And makes him bring back one leg.

[*One leg is a leg of mutton ; two legs, a man ; three legs,
a stool ; four legs, a dog.*

ELIZABETH, Elspeth, Betsy, and
    Bess,
They all went together to seek a bird's
    nest.
They found a bird's nest with five eggs in,
They all took one, and left four in.

THERE was a man of Thessaly,
    And he was wond'rous wise;
He jump'd into a quickset hedge,
    And scratch'd out both his eyes.
But when he saw his eyes were out,
    With all his might and main
He jump'd into another hedge,
    And scratch'd 'em in again.

I WOULD if I cou'd,
  If I cou'dn't, how cou'd I?
I cou'dn't, without I cou'd, cou'd I?
Cou'd you, without you cou'd, cou'd ye?
Cou'd ye, cou'd ye?
Cou'd you, without you cou'd, cou'd ye?

THREE children sliding on the ice
  Upon a summer's day,
As it fell out, they all fell in,
  The rest they ran away.

Now had these children been at home,
  Or sliding on dry ground,
Ten thousand pounds to one penny
  They had not all been drown'd.

You parents all that children have,
  And you that have got none,
If you would have them safe abroad,
  Pray keep them safe at home,

IF all the world was apple-pie,
   And all the sea was ink,
And all the trees were bread and cheese,
   What should we have for drink?

PETER WHITE will ne'er go right.
    Would you know the reason why?
He follows his nose where'er he goes,
    And that stands all awry.

THERE was a little Guinea-pig,
    Who, being little, was not big;
He always walked upon his feet,
And never fasted when he eat.

When from a place he ran away,
He never at that place did stay;
And while he ran, as I am told,
He ne'er stood still for young or old.

He often squeak'd and sometimes vi'lent,
And when he squeak'd he ne'er was silent;
Though ne'er instructed by a cat,
He knew a mouse was not a rat.

One day, as I am certified,
He took a whim and fairly died;
And, as I'm told by men of sense,
He never has been living since.

THE man in the wilderness asked me
   How many strawberries grew in the sea.
I answered him as I thought good,
As many as red herrings grew in the wood.

MY true love lives far from me,
    Perrie, Merrie, Dixie, Dominie.
Many a rich present he sends to me,
    Petrum, Partrum, Paradise, Temporie,
    Perrie, Merrie, Dixie, Dominie.

He sent me a goose without a bone;
He sent me a cherry without a stone.
    Petrum, &c.

He sent me a Bible no man could read;
He sent me a blanket without a thread.
    Petrum, &c.

How could there be a goose without a bone?
How could there be a cherry without a stone?
    Petrum, &c.

How could there be a Bible no man could read?
How could there be a blanket without a thread?
    Petrum, &c.

When the goose is in the egg-shell, there is no bone;
When the cherry is in the blossom, there is no stone.
    Petrum, &c.

When the Bible is in the press no man it can read ;
When the wool is on the sheep's back, there is no
 thread.
 Petrum, &c.

I SAW a ship a-sailing,
 A-sailing on the sea ;
And, oh ! it was all laden
 With pretty things for thee !

There were comfits in the cabin,
 And apples in the hold
The sails were made of silk,
 And the masts were made of gold.

The four-and-twenty sailors
 That stood between the decks,
Were four-and-twenty white mice
 With chains about their necks.

The captain was a duck,
 With a packet on his back ;
And when the ship began to move,
 The captain said, "Quack ! quack ! "

HERE am I, little jumping Joan.
When nobody's with me,
I'm always alone.

O THAT I was where I would be,
Then would I be where I am not!
But where I am there I must be,
And where I would be I cannot.

TOBACCO reek! tobacco reek!
  When you're well, 'twill make you sick.
Tobacco reek! tobacco reek!
'Twill make you well when you are sick.

THERE was an old woman, and what do you
  think?
She lived upon nothing but victuals and drink:
Victuals and drink were the chief of her diet;
This tiresome old woman could never be quiet.

[*Mind your punctuation.*]

I SAW a peacock with a fiery tail,
  I saw a blazing comet drop down hail,
I saw a cloud wrapped with ivy round,
I saw an oak creep upon the ground,
I saw a pismire swallow up a whale,
I saw the sea brimful of ale,
I saw a Venice glass full fifteen feet deep,
I saw a well full of men's tears that weep,

I saw red eyes all of a flaming fire,
I saw a house bigger than the moon and higher,
I saw the sun at twelve o'clock at night,
I saw the man that saw this wondrous sight.

THERE was a man and he was mad,
  And he jump'd into a pea-swad; [1]
The pea-swad was over-full,
So he jump'd into a roaring bull;
The roaring bull was over-fat,
So he jump'd into a gentleman's hat:
The gentleman's hat was over-fine,
So he jump'd into a bottle of wine;
The bottle of wine was over-dear,
So he jump'd into a bottle of beer;
The bottle of beer was over-thick,
So he jump'd into a club-stick;
The club-stick was over-narrow,
So he jump'd into a wheel-barrow;
The wheel-barrow began to crack,
So he jump'd on to a hay-stack;
The hay-stack began to blaze,
So he did nothing but cough and sneeze!

---

[1] The pod or shell of a pea.

CHARMS & LULLABIES

CUSHY cow bonny, let down thy milk,
 And I will give thee a gown of silk ;
A gown of silk and a silver tee,
If thou wilt let down thy milk to me.

IF you love me, pop and fly;
If you hate me, lie and die.

*[Said to pips placed in the fire; a species of
divination practised by children.*

PETER PIPER picked a peck
of pickled pepper;
A peck of pickled pepper Peter
Piper picked;

If Peter Piper picked a peck of pickled pepper,
Where's the peck of pickled pepper Peter Piper
    picked?

MATTHEW, Mark, Luke, and John,
    Guard the bed that I lay on!
  Four corners to my bed,
  Four angels round my head;
One to watch, one to pray,
And two to bear my soul away!

COME, butter, come,
    Come, butter, come!
Peter stands at the gate,
Waiting for a butter'd cake;
Come, butter, come!

BYE, baby bunting,
Daddy's gone a hunting,
To get a little hare's skin
To wrap a baby bunting in.

HUSHY baby, my doll, I pray you don't cry,
And I'll give you some bread and some milk
by-and-by;
Or perhaps you like custard, or maybe a tart,—
Then to either you're welcome, with all my whole
heart.

DANCE to your daddy,
My little babby;
Dance to your daddy,
My little lamb.

You shall have a fishy,
In a little dishy;
You shall have a fishy
When the boat comes in.

Hush·a·bye, Baby

HUSH-A-BYE, baby, on the tree top;
When the wind blows, the cradle will rock;
When the bough bends, the cradle will fall;
Down will come baby, bough, cradle, and all.

RABBIT, rabbit, rabbit-pie!
Come, my ladies, come and buy,
Else your babies they will cry.

149

HEY, my kitten, my kitten,
  And hey, my kitten, my deary!
Such a sweet pet as this
  Was neither far nor neary.

Here we go up, up, up,
  And here we go down, down, downy;
And here we go backwards and forwards,
  And here we go round, round, roundy.

YOUNG lambs to sell!
  Young lambs to sell!
If I'd as much money as I can tell,
I never would cry, Young lambs to sell!

ROCK-A-BYE, baby, thy cradle is green;
  Father's a nobleman, mother's a queen;
And Betty's a lady, and wears a gold ring;
And Johnny's a drummer, and drums for the king.

TO market, to market,
To buy a plum bun;
Home again, come again,
Market is done.

151

HICKUP, hickup, go away!
  Come again another day;
Hickup, hickup, when I bake,
I'll give to you a butter-cake.

HICKUP, snicup,
  Rise up, right up,
Three drops in the cup
Are good for the hiccup.

SWAN swam over the sea—
  Swim, swan, swim,
Swan swam back again,
  Well swam swan.

GAFFERS & GAMMERS

T HERE was an old woman
Lived under a hill,
And if she's not gone
She lives there still.

THERE was an old woman, as I've heard tell,
   She went to market her eggs for to sell;
She went to market all on a market-day,
And she fell asleep on the king's highway.

There came by a pedlar whose name was Stout;
He cut her petticoats all round about;
He cut her petticoats up to the knees,
Which made the old woman to shiver and freeze.

When this little woman first did wake,
She began to shiver and she began to shake;
She began to wonder and she began to cry,
"Oh! deary, deary me, this is none of I!

"But if it be I, as I do hope it be,
I've a little dog at home, and he'll know me;
If it be I, he'll wag his little tail,
And if it be not I, he'll loudly bark and wail."

Home went the little woman all in the dark;
Up got the little dog, and he began to bark;
He began to bark, so she began to cry,
"Oh! deary, deary me, this is none of I!"

OLD woman, old woman, shall we go a shearing?"
  "Speak a little louder, sir, I am very thick of
    hearing."
"Old woman, old woman, shall I love you dearly?"
"Thank you, kind sir, I hear you very clearly."

THERE was an old woman toss'd up in a
    basket
  Nineteen times as high as the moon;
Where she was going I couldn't but ask it,
  For in her hand she carried a broom.

"Old woman, old woman, old woman," quoth I,
  "O whither, O whither, O whither, so high?"
"To brush the cobwebs off the sky!"
  "Shall I go with thee?"   "Ay, by-and-by."

ALITTLE old man and I fell out;
  "How shall we bring this matter about?'
"Bring it about as well as you can;
Get you gone, you little old man!"

THERE was an old woman of Leeds
    Who spent all her time in good deeds;
She worked for the poor
Till her fingers were sore,
This pious old woman of Leeds!

THERE was an old woman
    Lived under a hill;
She put a mouse in a bag,
    And sent it to mill.

The miller declar'd
    By the point of his knife,
He never took toll
    Of a mouse in his life.

THERE was an old woman who lived in a shoe;
    She had so many children she didn't know what
        to do;
She gave them some broth without any bread;
She whipped them all soundly and put them to bed.

SHE HAD SO MANY CHILDREN SHE DIDN'T KNOW WHAT TO DO

THERE was an old woman had three sons,
　Jerry, and James, and John :
Jerry was hung, James was drowned,
John was lost and never was found,
And there was an end of the three sons,
Jerry, and James, and John !

THERE was an old man of Tobago,
　Who lived on rice, gruel, and sago,
Till, much to his bliss,
His physician said this—
"To a leg, sir, of mutton you may go."

THERE was an old woman of Norwich,
　Who lived upon nothing but porridge ;
Parading the town,
She turned cloak into gown,
This thrifty old woman of Norwich.

THERE was an old woman called Nothing-at-all,
    Who rejoiced in a dwelling exceedingly small ;
A man stretched his mouth to its utmost extent,
And down at one gulp house and old woman went.

THERE was an old man,
    And he had a calf,
    And that's half ;
He took him out of the stall,
, And put him on the wall ;
    And that's all.

OLD Betty Blue
    Lost a holiday shoe,
What can old Betty do ?
    Give her another
    To match the other,
And then she may swagger in two.

OLD Mother Hubbard
    Went to the cupboard
  To get her poor dog a bone;
But when she came there
The cupboard was bare,
    And so the poor dog had none.

She went to the baker's
    To buy him some bread,
But when she came back
    The poor dog was dead.

She went to the joiner's
    To buy him a coffin,
But when she came back
    The poor dog was laughing.

She took a clean dish
    To get him some tripe,
But when she came back
    He was smoking his pipe.

She went to the fishmonger's
    To buy him some fish.
And when she came back
    He was licking the dish.

She went to the ale-house
To get him some beer,
But when she came back
The dog sat in a chair.

She went to the tavern
For white wine and red,
But when she came back
The dog stood on his head.

She went to the hatter's
To buy him a hat,
But when she came back
He was feeding the cat.

She went to the barber's
To buy him a wig,
But when she came back
He was dancing a jig.

She went to the fruiterer's
To buy him some fruit,
But when she came back
He was playing the flute.

She went to the tailor's
To buy him a coat,
But when she came back
He was riding a goat.

She went to the cobbler's
　To buy him some shoes,
But when she came back
　He was reading the news.

She went to the sempstress
　To buy him some linen,
But when she came back
　The dog was spinning.

She went to the hosier's
　To buy him some hose,
But when she came back
　He was dress'd in his clothes

The dame made a curtsey,
　The dog made a bow;
The dame said, "Your servant,"
　The dog said, "Bow, wow."

GAMES

THERE were three jovial Welshmen,
  As I have heard them say,
And they would go a-hunting
  Upon St. David's day.

All the day they hunted,
  And nothing could they find
But a ship a-sailing,
  A-sailing with the wind.

Y

One said it was a ship;
 The other he said nay;
The third said it was a house,
 With the chimney blown away.

And all the night they hunted,
 And nothing could they find
But the moon a-gliding,
 A-gliding with the wind.

One said it was the moon;
 The other he said nay;
The third said it was a cheese,
 And half o't cut away.

And all the day they hunted,
 And nothing could they find
But a hedgehog in a bramble-bush,
 And that they left behind.

The first said it was a hedgehog;
 The second he said nay;
The third it was a pin-cushion,
 And the pins stuck in wrong way.

And all the night they hunted,
   And nothing could they find
But a hare in a turnip field,
   And that they left behind.

The first said it was a hare;
   The second he said nay;
The third said it was a calf,
   And the cow had run away.

And all the day they hunted,
   And nothing could they find
But an owl in a holly-tree,
   And that they left behind.

One said it was an owl;
   The other he said nay;
The third said 'twas an old man,
   And his beard growing grey.

JACK, be nimble,
   And, Jack, be quick;
And, Jack, jump over
   The candlestick.

QUEEN ANNE, Queen Anne, you sit in the sun,
    As fair as a lily, as white as a wand.
I send you three letters, and pray read one;
You must read one, if you can't read all;
So pray, Miss or Master, throw up the ball.

[*Children hunting bats.*]

BAT, bat (*clap hands*),
    Come under my hat,
    And I'll give you a slice of bacon;
And when I bake,
I'll give you a cake,
    If I am not mistaken.

[*At the conclusion, the captive is privately asked if he will have oranges or lemons (the two leaders of the arch having previously agreed which designation shall belong to each), and he goes behind the one he may chance to name. When all are thus divided into two parties, they conclude the game by trying to pull each other beyond a certain line.*]

GAY go up and gay go down,
    To ring the bells of London town.

Bull's eyes and targets,
Say the bells of St. Marg'ret's.

Brickbats and tiles,
Say the bells of St. Giles'.

Halfpence and farthings,
Say the bells of St. Martin's.

Oranges and lemons,
Say the bells of St. Clement's.

Pancakes and fritters,
Say the bells of St. Peter's.

Two sticks and an apple,
Say the bells at Whitechapel.

Old Father Baldpate,
Say the slow bells at Aldgate.

You owe me ten shillings,
Say the bells at St. Helen's.

Pokers and tongs,
Say the bells at St. John's.

Kettles and pans,
Say the bells at St. Ann's.

When will you pay me?
Say the bells at Old Bailey.

When I grow rich,
Say the bells at Shoreditch.

Pray when will that be?
Say the bells of Stepney.

I am sure I don't know,
Says the great bell at Bow.

Here comes a candle to light you to bed,
And here comes a chopper to chop off your head.

[*Game on a child's features.*]

HERE sits the Lord Mayor;   [*Forehead.*
    Here sit his two men;   [*Eyes.*
Here sits the cock;   [*Right cheek.*
    Here sits the hen;   [*Left cheek.*
Here sit the little chickens;   [*Tip of nose.*
    Here they run in,   [*Mouth.*
Chinchopper, chinchopper,
    Chinchopper, chin!   [*Chuck the chin.*

DANCE, Thumbkin, dance;
          [*Keep the thumb in motion.*
Dance, ye merrymen, every one;
          [*All the fingers in motion.*
For Thumbkin, he can dance alone,
          [*The thumb only moving.*
Thumbkin, he can dance alone;   [*Ditto.*
Dance, Foreman, dance,   [*The first finger moving.*
Dance, ye merrymen, every one;
          [*The whole moving.*
But, Foreman, he can dance alone,
Foreman, he can dance alone.

[*And so on with the others, naming the second finger " Longman," the third finger " Ringman," and the fourth finger " Littleman." Littleman cannot dance alone.*]

[*Children stand round, and are counted one by one, by means of this rhyme. The child upon whom the last number falls is out, for " Hide or Seek," or any other game where a victim is required.*]

HICKORY (1), Dickory (2), Dock (3),
    The mouse ran up the clock (4);
The clock struck one (5);
The mouse was gone (6);
O (7), U (8), T (9), spells OUT!

[*A game at ball.*]

CUCKOO, cherry-tree,
    Catch a bird, and give it to me;
Let the tree be high or low,
Let it hail, rain, or snow.

[*A song set to five fingers.*]

1. THIS pig went to market;
    2. This pig stayed at home;
3. This pig had a bit of meat,
4. And this pig had none;
5. This pig said, "Wee, wee, wee!
    I can't find my way home."

THE FIVE PIGS

z

[A play with the face.   The child exclaims :]

RING the bell!   *[Giving a lock of its hair a pull.*
   Knock at the door!   *[Tapping its forehead.*
Draw the latch!   *[Pulling up its nose.*
And walk in!   *[Opening its mouth and putting in its finger.*

[Game with the hands.]

PEASE-PUDDING hot,
   Pease-pudding cold,
Pease-pudding in the pot,
   Nine days old.
Some like it hot,
   Some like it cold,
Some like it in the pot,
   Nine days old.

IS John Smith within?"—
   "Yes, that he is."
"Can he set a shoe?"—
"Ay, marry, two,
Here a nail, there a nail,
Tick, tack, too."

1. I WENT up one pair of stairs.
  2. Just like me.
1. I went up two pair of stairs.
  2. Just like me.
1. I went into a room.
  2. Just like me.
1. I looked out of a window.
  2. Just like me.
1. And there I saw a monkey.
  2. Just like me.

1. I AM a gold lock.
  2. I am a gold key.
1. I am a silver lock.
  2. I am a silver key.
1. I am a brass lock.
  2. I am a brass key.
1. I am a lead lock.
  2. I am a lead key.
1. I am a monk lock.
  2. I am a monk key !

Suitors.

WE are three brethren out of Spain,
    Come to court your daughter Jane.

Mother.

My daughter Jane she is too young,
And has not learned her mother-tongue.

Suitors.

Be she young, or be she old,
For her beauty she must be sold.
So fare you well, my lady gay,
We'll call again another day.

Mother.

Turn back, turn back, thou scornful knight,
And rub thy spurs till they be bright.

Suitors.

Of my spurs take you no thought,
For in this town they were not bought;
So fare you well, my lady gay,
We'll call again another day.

Mother.

Turn back, turn back, thou scornful knight,
And take the fairest in your sight.

Suitor.

The fairest maid that I can see,
Is pretty Nancy—come to me.

Here comes your daughter safe and sound,
Every pocket with a thousand pound,
Every finger with a gay gold ring.
Please to take your daughter in.

R IDE a cock-horse to Banbury Cross,
    To buy little Johnny a galloping-horse;
It trots behind, and it ambles before,
And Johnny shall ride till he can ride no more.

R IDE a cock-horse to Banbury Cross,
    To see what Tommy can buy;
A penny white loaf, a penny white cake,
    And a twopenny apple-pie.

[*The following is a game played thus: A string of boys and girls, each holding by his predecessor's skirts, approaches two others, who with joined and elevated hands form a double arch. After the dialogue, the line passes through, and the last is caught by a sudden lowering of the arms—if possible.*] ·

HOW many miles is it to Babylon?"—
      "Threescore miles and ten."
"Can I get there by candle-light?"—
"Yes, and back again!
If your heels are nimble and light,
You may get there by candle-light."

R IDE a cock-horse to Banbury Cross,
To see an old lady upon a white horse;
Rings on her fingers, and bells on her toes,
And so she makes music wherever she goes.

[*A string of children, hand in hand, stand in a row. A child* (A) *stands in front of them, as leader; two other children* (B *and* C) *form an arch, each holding both the hands of the other.*]

A. D RAW a pail of water
For my lady's daughter.
My father's a king, and my mother's a queen;
My two little sisters are dress'd in green,
Stamping grass and parsley,
Marigold leaves and daisies.

One rush, two rush,
Pray thee, fine lady, come under my bush.

[A *passes by under the arch, followed by the whole string of children, the last of whom is taken captive by* B *and* C. *The verses are repeated, until all are taken.*]

S EE-SAW sacradown,
Which is the way to London town?
One foot up and the other down,
And that is the way to London town.

SEE, saw, Margery Daw
   Sold her bed and lay upon straw.
Was not she a dirty slut,
To sell her bed and lie in the dirt!

SEE, saw, Margery Daw,
   Little Jackey shall have a new master;
Little Jackey shall have but a penny a day,
   Because he can't work any faster.

[The following is used by schoolboys, when two are starting to run a race.]

ONE to make ready,
  And two to prepare;
Good luck to the rider,
  And away goes the mare.

[A game on the slate.]

EGGS, butter, bread,
  Stick, stock, stone dead!
Stick him up, stick him down,
Stick him in the old man's crown!

WHO goes round my house this night?
  None but bloody Tom!
Who steals all the sheep at night?
None but this poor one.

WHOOP, whoop, and hollow,
  Good dogs won't follow,
Without the hare cries " Pee-wit."

THIS is the way the ladies
    ride :
   Tri, tre, tre, tree,
   Tri, tre, tre, tree !
This is the way the ladies ride :
   Tri, tre, tre, tre, tri-tre-tre-
    tree !

This is the way the gentlemen
    ride :
   Gallop-a-trot,
   Gallop-a-trot !
This is the way the gentlemen
    ride :
   Gallop-a-gallop-a-trot !

This is the way the farmers
    ride :
   Hobbledy-hoy,
   Hobbledy-hoy !
This is the way the farmers
    ride :
   Hobbledy hobbledy-hoy !

"HERE stands a post.
     Who put it there?"
"A better man than you:
Touch it if you dare!"

THERE were two blackbirds
     Sitting on a hill,
The one nam'd Jack,
     The other nam'd Jill.
     Fly away Jack!
     Fly away Jill!
     Come again Jack!
     Come again Jill!

JINGLES

DEEDLE, deedle, dumpling, my son John
Went to bed with his trousers on ;
One shoe off, the other shoe on,
Deedle, deedle, dumpling, my son John.

COCK-a-doodle-doo!
  My dame has lost her shoe;
My master's lost his fiddling-stick,
And don't know what to do.

Cock-a-doodle-doo!
What is my dame to do?
Till master finds his fiddling-stick,
She'll dance without her shoe.

Cock-a-doodle-doo!
My dame has lost her shoe,
And master's found his fiddling-stick;
Sing doodle-doodle-doo!

Cock-a-doodle-doo!
My dame will dance with you,
While master fiddles his fiddling-stick,
For dame and doodle-doo.

Cock-a-doodle-doo!
Dame has lost her shoe;
Gone to bed and scratch'd her head,
And can't tell what to do.

HEY! diddle, diddle,
    The cat and the fiddle,
The cow jumped over the moon;
    The little dog laugh'd
    To see the sport,
While the dish ran after the spoon.

PUSSICAT, wussicat, with a white foot,
    When is your wedding? for I'll come to't.
The beer's to brew, the bread's to bake,
Pussy-cat, pussy-cat, don't be too late.

DING, dong, bell,
    Pussy's in the well!
Who put her in?—
Little Tommy Lin.
Who pulled her out?—
Dog with long snout.
What a naughty boy was that
To drown poor pussy-cat,
Who never did any harm,
But kill'd the mice in his father's barn.

DIDDLEDY, diddledy, dumpty;
    The cat ran up the plum-tree.
I'll lay you a crown
I'll fetch you down;
So diddledy, diddledy, dumpty.

FIDDLE-DE-DEE, fiddle-de-dee,
   The fly shall marry the humble-bee.
They went to the church, and married was she:
The fly has married the humble-bee.

🏵

TO market, to market, to buy a fat pig;
   Home again, home again, dancing a jig.
Ride to the market to buy a fat hog;
   Home again, home again, jiggety-jog.

HANDY SPANDY, Jack-a-dandy,
 Loved plum-cake and sugar-candy;
He bought some at a grocer's shop,
And out he came, hop, hop, hop.

TWEEDLE-DUM and Tweedle-dee
 Resolved to have a battle
For Tweedle-dum said Tweedle-dee
 Had spoiled his nice new rattle.

Just then flew by a monstrous crow
 As big as a tar-barrel,
Which frightened both the heroes so
 They quite forgot their quarrel.

RUB a dub dub,
 Three men in a tub:
And who do you think they be?
The butcher, the baker,
The candlestick-maker;
Turn 'em out, knaves all three!

LOVE &
MATRIMONY

J ACK and Jill went up the hill
  To fetch a pail of water;
Jack fell down and broke his crown,
  And Jill came tumbling after.

ROSEMARY green,
And lavender blue,
Thyme and sweet marjoram,
Hyssop and rue.

BRAVE news is come to town;
Brave news is carried;
Brave news is come to town
Jemmy Dawson's married.

SYLVIA, sweet as morning air,
Do not drive me to despair:
Long have I sighed in vain,
Now I am come again:
Will you be mine or no, no-a-no,—
Will you be mine or no?

Simon, pray leave off your suit,
For of your courting you'll reap no fruit.
I would rather give a crown
Than be married to a clown;
Go for a booby, go, no-a-no,—
Go, for a booby, go.

THERE was a little boy and a little girl
    Lived in an alley;
Says the little boy to the little girl,
  "Shall I, oh! shall I?"

Says the little girl to the little boy,
　"What shall we do?"
Says the little boy to the little girl,
　"I will kiss you."

WHEN I was a bachelor I lived by myself,
　　And all the meat I got I put upon a shelf;
The rats and the mice did lead me such a life
That I went to London to get myself a wife.

The streets were so broad and the lanes were so
　　narrow,
I could not get my wife home without a wheel-
　　barrow;
The wheelbarrow broke, my wife got a fall,
Down tumbled wheelbarrow, little wife, and all.

BLUE eye beauty,
　Grey eye greedy,
Black eye blackie,
Brown eye brownie.

AS Tommy Snooks and Bessy Brooks
    Were walking out one Sunday,
Says Tommy Snooks to Bessy Brooks,
    "To-morrow will be Monday."

OH, madam, I will give you the keys of
Canterbury,
To set all the bells ringing when we shall be
merry,
If you will but walk abroad with me,
If you will but walk with me.

Sir, I'll not accept of the keys of Canterbury,
To set all the bells ringing when we shall be
merry;
Neither will I walk abroad with thee,
Neither will I talk with thee!

Oh, madam, I will give you a fine carved comb,
To comb out your ringlets when I am from
home,
If you will but walk with me, &c.
Sir, I'll not accept, &c.

Oh, madam, I will give you a pair of shoes of
cork,
One made in London, the other made in York,
If you will but walk with me, &c.
Sir, I'll not accept, &c.

Madam, I will give you a sweet silver bell,
To ring up your maidens when you are not well,
If you will but walk with me, &c.
Sir, I'll not accept, &c.

Oh, my man John, what can the matter be?
I love the lady and the lady loves not me!
Neither will she walk abroad with me,
Neither will she talk with me.

Oh, master dear, do not despair,
The lady she shall be, shall be your only dear;
And she will walk and talk with thee,
And she will walk with thee!

Oh, madam, I will give you the keys of my chest,
To count my gold and silver when I am gone to rest,
If you will but walk abroad with me,
If you will but talk with me.

Oh, sir, I will accept of the keys of your chest,
To count your gold and silver when you are gone
     to rest,
And I will walk abroad with thee,
And I will talk with thee!

JACK in the pulpit, out and in,
Sold his wife for a minikin pin.

JACK SPRAT could eat no fat,
His wife could eat no lean :

And so, betwixt them both, you see,
    They lick'd the platter clean.

BESSY BELL and Mary Gray,
    They were two bonny lasses;
They built their house upon the lea,
    And covered it with rashes.

Bessy kept the garden gate,
    And Mary kept the pantry;
Bessy always had to wait,
    While Mary lived in plenty.

THERE was a little man,
    And he woo'd a little maid,
And he said, " Little maid, will you wed, wed, wed ?
    I have little more to say,
    Than will you, yea or nay,
For least said is soonest mended-ded, ded, ded."

    The little maid replied,
    Some say a little sighed,
" But what shall we have for to eat, eat, eat ?
    Will the love that you're so rich in
    Make a fire in the kitchen ?
Or the little god of love turn the spit, spit, spit ? "

UP hill and down dale,
    Butter is made in every vale,
And if that Nancy Cook
Is a good girl,
She shall have a spouse,
And make butter anon,
Before her old grandmother
Grows a young man.

AS I was going up Pippen-hill,
   Pippen-hill was dirty
There I met a pretty miss,
   And she dropt me a curtsey.

Little miss, pretty miss,
  Blessings light upon you!
If I had half-a-crown a day
  I'd spend it all on you.

HERE comes a lusty wooer,
  My a dildin, my a daldin;
Here comes a lusty wooer,
  Lily bright and shine a'.

" Pray, who do you woo,
  My a dildin, my a daldin?
Pray, who do you woo,
  Lily bright and shine a'?"

"For your fairest daughter,
  My a dildin, my a daldin;
For your fairest daughter,
  Lily bright and shine a'."

" Then there she is for you,
  My a dildin, my a daldin;
Then there she is for you,
  Lily bright and shine a'. "

HERE COMES A LUSTY WOOER

MASTER I have, and I am his man,
Gallop a dreary dun;
Master I have, and I am his man,
And I'll get a wife as fast as I can;
With a heighly gaily gamberally,
Higgledy piggledy, niggledy, niggledy,
Gallop a dreary dun.

I HAD a little husband,
No bigger than my thumb;
I put him in a pint pot,
And there I bid him drum.

I bought a little horse,
That galloped up and down;
I bridled him, and saddled him,
And sent him out of town.

I gave him some garters
To garter up his hose,
And a little handkerchief
To wipe his pretty nose

DID you see my wife, did you see, did you see,
  Did you see my wife looking for me?
She wears a straw bonnet, with white ribbands on it,
  And dimity petticoats over her knee.

I DOUBT, I doubt, my fire is out;
  My little wife isn't at home;
I'll saddle my dog, and I'll bridle my cat,
  And I'll go fetch my little wife home.

LOVE your own, kiss your own,
  Love your own mother, hinny,
For if she was dead and gone,
  You'd ne'er get such another, hinny.

CURLY locks! curly locks! wilt thou be mine?
  Thou shalt not wash dishes, nor yet feed the
    swine,
But sit on a cushion and sew a fine seam,
And feed upon strawberries, sugar, and cream!

GEORGEY PORGEY, pudding and pie,
Kissed the girls and made them cry;
When the girls come out to play,
Georgey Porgey runs away.

THERE was a lady loved a swine:
"Honey," quoth she,
"Pig-hog, wilt thou be mine?"
"Grunt," quoth he.

"I'll build thee a silver stye,
Honey," quoth she;
"And in it thou shalt lie;"
"Grunt," quoth he.

"Pinned with a silver pin,
Honey," quoth she,
"That you may go out and in;"
"Grunt," quoth he.

"Wilt thou now have me,
Honey," quoth she;
"Grunt, grunt, grunt," quoth he,
And went his way.

WHERE have you been all the day,
      My boy Willy?"
"I've been all the day
Courting of a lady gay:
But, oh! she's too young
To be taken from her mammy."

"What work can she do,
      My boy Willy?
Can she bake and can she brew,
      My boy Willy?"
"She can brew and she can bake,
And she can make our wedding-cake:
But, oh! she's too young
To be taken from her mammy."

"What age may she be?   What age may she be?
      My boy Willy?"
"Twice two, twice seven,
Twice ten, twice eleven:
But, oh! she's too young
To be taken from her mammy."

NATURAL HISTORY

I HAD a little dog, and they called him Buff;
  I sent him to the shop for a hap'orth of snuff;
But he lost the bag, and spill'd the snuff:
"So take that cuff—and that's enough."

BURNIE bee, burnie bee,
  Tell me when your wedding be?
If it be to-morrow day,
Take your wings and fly away.

SOME little mice sat in a barn to spin;
  Pussy came by, and popped her head in;
"Shall I come in and cut your threads off?"
"Oh no, kind sir, you will snap our heads off?"

ALL of a row,
  Bend the bow,
Shot at a pigeon,
And killed a crow.

GREY goose and gander,
  Waft your wings together,
And carry the good king's daughter
Over the one strand river.

P USSY-CAT, pussy-cat, where have you been?
     I've been up to London to look at the queen.
Pussy-cat, pussy-cat, what did you there?
I frighten'd a little mouse under the chair.

CUCKOO, Cuckoo,
What do you do?
" In April
I open my bill;
In May
I sing night and day;
In June
I change my tune;
In July
Away I fly;
In August
Away I must."

HICKETY, pickety, my black hen,
She lays eggs for gentlemen;
Gentlemen come every day
To see what my black hen doth lay.

THE cock doth crow,
To let you know,
If you be wise,
'Tis time to rise.

R OBERT BARNES, fellow fine,
Can you shoe this horse of mine?
" Yes, good sir, that I can,
As well as any other man:
There's a nail, and there's a prod,
And now, good sir, your horse is shod."

[*Bird boy's song.*]

E AT, birds, eat, and make no waste;
I lie here and make no haste:
If my master chance to come,
You must fly, and I must run.

H IE hie," says Anthony,
" Puss in the pantry,
Gnawing, gnawing
A mutton mutton-bone;
See now she tumbles it,
See now she mumbles it,
See how she tosses
The mutton mutton-bone."

FOUR and twenty tailors went to kill a snail ;
The best man among them durst not touch
her tail.

She put out her horns like a little Kyloe cow;
Run, tailors, run, or she'll kill you all e'en now.

THE cuckoo's a fine bird :
    He sings as he flies ;
He brings us good tidings ;
    He tells us no lies.

He sucks little birds' eggs
    To make his voice clear ;
And when he sings " Cuckoo ! "
    The summer is near.

CROAK ! " said the Toad, " I'm hungry, I think ;
    To-day I've had nothing to eat or to drink ;
I'll crawl to a garden and jump through the pales,
And there I'll dine nicely on slugs and on snails."
" Ho, ho ! " quoth the Frog, " is that what you mean ?
Then I'll hop away to the next meadow stream ;
There I will drink, and eat worms and slugs too,
And then I shall have a good dinner like you."

2 F

THERE was a piper, he'd a cow,
And he'd no hay to give her;
He took his pipes and played a tune:
"Consider, old cow, consider!"

The cow considered very well,
  For she gave the piper a penny,
That he might play the tune again,
  Of "Corn rigs are bonnie."

A PIE sate on a pear-tree,
  A pie sate on a pear-tree,
A pie sate on a pear-tree.
Heigh O, heigh O, heigh O!
Once so merrily hopp'd she,
Twice so merrily hopp'd she,
Thrice so merrily hopp'd she.
Heigh O, heigh O, heigh O!

ONCE I saw a little bird
  Come hop, hop, hop;
So I cried, "Little bird,
Will you stop, stop, stop?"
And was going to the window,
To say, "How do you do?"
But he shook his little tail,
And far away he flew.

THE winds they did blow;
   The leaves they did wag;
Along came a beggar boy,
   And put me in his bag.

He took me up to London;
   A lady did me buy,
Put me in a silver cage,
   And hung me up on high,

With apples by the fire,
   And nuts for to crack,
Besides a little feather bed
   To rest my little back.

COCK ROBIN got up early
   At the break of day,
And went to Jenny's window,
   To sing a roundelay.

He sang Cock Robin's love
   To the pretty Jenny Wren;
And when he got unto the end,
   Then he began again.

BETTY PRINGLE had a little pig,
   Not very little and not very big;
When he was alive he lived in clover;
But now he's dead, and that's all over.
So Billy Pringle he laid down and cried,
And Betty Pringle she laid down and died;
So there was an end of one, two, and three:
Billy Pringle he,
Betty Pringle she,
And the piggy wiggy.

A LONG-TAIL'D pig, or a short-tail'd pig,
   Or a pig without e'er a tail,
A sow-pig, or a boar-pig,
   Or a pig with a curly tail.

A LITTLE cock-sparrow sat on a green tree
(*tris*),
And he cherruped, he cherruped, so merry was he
(*tris*);
A little cock-sparrow sat on a green tree,
And he cherruped, he cherruped, so merry was he.

A naughty boy came with his wee bow and arrow
(*tris*),
Determined to shoot this little cock-sparrow (*tris*);
A naughty, &c.
Determined, &c.

"This little cock-sparrow shall make me a stew (*tris*),
And his giblets shall make me a little pie too " (*tris*);
" Oh, no," said the sparrow, " I *won't* make a
stew ; "
So he flapped his wings, and away he flew.

LITTLE Robin Red-Breast
Sat upon a rail :
Niddle-naddle went his head !
Wiggle-waggle went his tail.

DAME, what makes your ducks to die?
What the pize ails 'em? what the pize ails
'em?
They kick up their heels, and there they lie;
What the pize ails 'em now?
Heigh, ho! heigh, ho!
Dame, what makes your ducks to die?
What a pize ails 'em? what a pize ails 'em?
Heigh, ho! heigh, ho!
Dame, what ails your ducks to die?
Eating o' polly-wigs, eating o' polly-wigs.
Heigh, ho! heigh, ho!

IN the month of February,
  When green leaves begin to spring,
Little lambs do skip like fairies,
  Birds do couple, build, and sing.

PUSSY CAT sits by the fire;
  How did she come there?
In walks the little dog,
  Says, " Pussy! are you there?"

" How do you do, Mistress Pussy?
  Mistress Pussy, how d'ye do?"
" I thank you kindly, little dog,
  I fare as well as you!"

THERE was a little boy went into a barn,
  And lay down on some hay;
An owl came out and flew about,
  And the little boy ran away.

THE dove says, "Coo, coo, what shall I do?
    I can scarce maintain two."
"Pooh, pooh," says the wren; "I have got ten,
And keep them all like gentlemen!"

BOW, wow, wow,
    Whose dog art thou?
"Little Tom Tinker's dog,
    Bow, wow, wow."

2 G

LEG over leg,
    As the dog went to Dover;
When he came to a stile,
    Jump he went over.

I LOVE little pussy, her coat is so warm;
    And if I don't hurt her she'll do me no harm.
So I'll not pull her tail nor drive her away,
But pussy and I very gently will play.

[*Imitated from a pigeon.*]

CURR dhoo, curr dhoo,
  Love me, and I'll love you!

LADY bird, lady bird, fly away home;
  Thy house is on fire, thy children all gone—
All but one, and her name is Ann,
And she crept under the pudding-pan.

PUSSY sits behind the fire—
How can she be fair?
In comes the little dog:
"Pussy, are you there?
"So, so, Mistress Pussy,
Pray how do you do?"
"Thank you, thank you, little dog,
I'm very well just now."

LITTLE Robin-Redbreast sat upon a tree;
Up went Pussy cat, and down went he;
Down came Pussy cat, and away Robin ran:
Says little Robin-Redbreast, "Catch me if you can."
Little Robin-Redbreast jump'd upon a wall;
Pussy cat jump'd after him, and almost got a fall;
Little Robin chirp'd and sang, and what did Pussy say?
Pussy cat said "Mew," and Robin jump'd away.

MARY had a pretty bird
With feathers bright and yellow—
Slender legs—upon my word—
He was a pretty fellow.

I HAD a little hen, the prettiest ever seen;
  She washed me the dishes, and kept the house
    clean;
She went to the mill to fetch me some flour;
She brought it home in less than an hour;
She baked me my bread, she brew'd me my ale;
She sat by the fire, and told many a fine tale.

HIGGLEY Piggley,
　My black hen,
She lays eggs
　For gentlemen ;
Sometimes nine,
　And sometimes ten.
Higgley Piggley,
　My black hen !

238

COME, take up your hats, and away let us haste
    To the Butterfly's ball, and the Grasshopper's
       feast ;
The trumpeter, Gad-fly, has summoned the crew,
And the revels are now only waiting for you.
On the smooth-shaven grass, by the side of a wood,
Beneath a broad oak which for ages had stood,
See the children of earth, and the tenants of air,
To an evening's amusement together repair.
And there came the Beetle, so blind and so black,
Who carried the Emmet, his friend, on his back ;
And there came the Gnat and the Dragon-fly too,
With all their relations, green, orange, and blue.
And there came the Moth, with her plumage of
      down,
And the Hornet with jacket of yellow and brown ;
And with him the Wasp, his companion, did bring ;
But they promised that evening to lay by their sting.
Then the sly little Dormouse peeped out of his hole,
And led to the feast his blind cousin the Mole ;
And the Snail, with her horns peeping out of her
      shell,
Came, fatigued with the distance, the length of an ell.
A mushroom the table, and on it was spread
A water-dock leaf, which their table-cloth made.

The viands were various, to each of their taste,
And the Bee brought the honey to sweeten the
feast.
With steps most majestic the Snail did advance,
And he promised the gazers a minuet to dance;
But they all laughed so loud that he drew in his
head,
And went in his own little chamber to bed.
Then, as evening gave way to the shadows of night,
Their watchman, the Glow-worm, come out with
his light.
So home let us hasten, while yet we can see,
For no watchman is waiting for you or for me.

BAH, bah, black sheep,
Have you any wool?
"Yes, marry, have I,
Three bags full:
One for my master,
And one for my dame,
But none for the little boy
Who cries in the lane."

LITTLE boy blue, come, blow up your horn;
  The sheep's in the meadow, the cow's in the
    corn.

2 H

" Where's the little boy that looks after the sheep ? "
" He's under the hay-cock fast asleep."
" Will you wake him ? "   " No, not I ;
For if I do, he'll be sure to cry."

GOD bless the master of this house,
The mistress bless also,
And all the little children
   That round the table go ;

And all your kin and kinsmen,
   That dwell both far and near ;
I wish you a merry Christmas,
   And a happy New Year.

LITTLE girl, little girl, where have you been ?
   " Gathering roses to give to the queen."

" Little girl, little girl, what gave she you ? "
" She gave me a diamond as big as my shoe."

GOOSEY, goosey, gander,
   Where shall I wander?
Upstairs, downstairs,
   And in my lady's chamber.
There I meet an old man
   That would not say his prayers;
I took him by the left leg,
   And threw him downstairs.

JENNY Wren fell sick,
  Upon a merry time;
In came Robin-Redbreast
  And brought her sops and wine.

" Eat well of the sops, Jenny,
  Drink well of the wine."
" Thank you, Robin, kindly,
  You shall be mine."

Jenny she got well,
  And stood upon her feet,
And told Robin plainly
  She loved him not a bit.

Robin, being angry,
  Hopped upon a twig,
Saying, " Out upon you.   Fie upon you.
  Bold-faced jig."

THE hart he loves the high wood,
  The hare she loves the hill,
The knight he loves his bright sword,
  The lady—loves her will.

I HAD a little pony,
His name was Dapple-grey
I lent him to a lady,
To ride a mile away.
She whipped him, she slashed him,
She rode him through the mire;
I would not lend my pony now
For all the lady's hire.

A FARMER went trotting
    Upon his grey mare;
Bumpety, bumpety, bump!
With his daughter behind him,
    So rosy and fair;
Lumpety, lumpety, lump!

A raven cried "Croak;"
    And they all tumbled down;
Bumpety, bumpety, bump!
The mare broke her knees,
    And the farmer his crown;
Lumpety, lumpety, lump.

The mischievous raven
    Flew laughing away;
Bumpety, bumpety, bump!
And vowed he would serve them
    The same the next day;
Bumpety, bumpety, bump!

ACCUMULATIVE
STORIES

THIS is the house that Jack built.

2. This is the malt
That lay in the house that Jack built.

3. This is the rat,
That ate the malt,
That lay in the house that Jack built.

4. This is the cat,
   That kill'd the rat,
   That ate the malt,
   That lay in the house that Jack built.

5. This is the dog,
   That worried the cat,
   That kill'd the rat,
   That ate the malt,
   That lay in the house that Jack built.

6. This is the cow with the crumpled horn,
   That toss'd the dog,
   That worried the cat,
   That kill'd the rat,
   That ate the malt,
   That lay in the house that Jack built.

7. This is the maiden all forlorn,
   That milk'd the cow with the crumpled horn,
   That tossed the dog,
   That worried the cat,
   That kill'd the rat,
   That ate the malt,
   That lay in the house that Jack built.

8. This is the man all tatter'd and torn,
    That kissed the maiden all forlorn,
    That milk'd the cow with the crumpled horn,
    That tossed the dog,
    That worried the cat,
    That kill'd the rat,
    That ate the malt,
    That lay in the house that Jack built.

9. This is the priest all shaven and shorn,
    That married the man all tatter'd and torn,
    That kiss'd the maiden all forlorn,
    That milk'd the cow with the crumpled horn,
    That tossed the dog,
    That worried the cat,
    That kill'd the rat,
    That ate the malt,
    That lay in the house that Jack built.

10. This is the cock that crow'd in the morn,
    That waked the priest all shaven and shorn,
    That married the man all tatter'd and torn,
    That kiss'd the maiden all forlorn,
    That milk'd the cow with the crumpled horn,
    That tossed the dog,

That worried the cat,
That kill'd the rat,
That ate the malt,
That lay in the house that Jack built.

11. This is the farmer sowing his corn,
　　That kept the cock that crow'd in the
　　　　morn,
　　That waked the priest all shaven and shorn,
　　That married the man all tatter'd and torn,
　　That kissed the maiden all forlorn,
　　That milk'd the cow with the crumpled
　　　　horn,
　　That tossed the dog,
　　That worried the cat,
　　That kill'd the rat,
　　That ate the malt,
　　That lay in the house that Jack built.

AN old woman was sweeping her house, and she found a little crooked sixpence. "What," said she, "shall I do with this little sixpence? I will go to market, and buy a little pig."

As she was coming home, she came to a stile; but the pig would not go over the stile.

She went a little farther, and she met a dog. So she said to the dog—

> "Dog, dog, bite pig!
>   Pig won't get over the stile;
>   And I shan't get home to-night."

But the dog would not.

She went a little farther, and she met a stick. So she said—

> "Stick, stick, beat dog!
>   Dog won't bite pig?
>   Pig won't get over the stile,
>   And I shan't get home to-night."

But the stick would not.

She went a little farther, and she met a fire. So she said—

> "Fire, fire, burn stick!
>   Stick won't beat dog;

Dog won't bite pig;
Pig won't get over the stile,
And I shan't get home to-night."

But the fire would not.
She went a little farther, and she met some water.
So she said—

" Water, water, quench fire!
Fire won't burn stick;
Stick won't beat dog;
Dog won't bite pig;
Pig won't get over the stile,
And I shan't get home to-night."

But the water would not.
She went a little farther, and she met an ox.   So
she said—

" Ox, ox, drink water!
Water won't quench fire;
Fire won't burn stick;
Stick won't beat dog;
Dog won't bite pig;
Pig won't get over the stile,
And I shan't get home to-night."

THE OLD WOMAN AND HER PIG

But the ox would not.

She went a little farther, and she met a butcher.
So she said—

> " Butcher, butcher, kill ox !
>   Ox won't drink water ;
>   Water won't quench fire ;
>   Fire won't burn stick ;
>   Stick won't beat dog ;
>   Dog won't bite pig ;
>   Pig won't get over the stile,
>   And I shan't get home to-night."

But the butcher would not.

She went a little farther, and she met a rope.   So
she said—

> " Rope, rope, hang butcher !
>   Butcher won't kill ox ;
>   Ox won't drink water ;
>   Water won't quench fire ;
>   Fire won't burn stick ;
>   Stick won't beat dog ;
>   Dog won't bite pig ;
>   Pig won't get over the stile,
>   And I shan't get home to-night."

But the rope would not.

She went a little farther, and she met a rat.   So she said—

> " Rat, rat, gnaw rope !
> Rope won't hang butcher ;
> Butcher won't kill ox ;
> Ox won't drink water ;
> Water won't quench fire ;
> Fire won't burn stick ;
> Stick won't beat dog ;
> Dog won't bite pig ;
> Pig won't get over the stile,
> And I shan't get home to-night."

But the rat would not.

She went a little farther, and she met a cat.   So she said—

> " Cat, cat, kill rat ;
> Rat won't gnaw rope ;
> Rope won't hang butcher ;
> Butcher won't kill ox ;
> Ox won't drink water ;
> Water won't quench fire ;

Fire won't burn stick;
Stick won't beat dog;
Dog won't bite pig;
Pig won't get over the stile,
And I shan't get home to-night."

The cat said, "If you will give me a saucer of milk, I will kill the rat."

So the old woman gave the cat the milk, and when she had lapped up the milk—

The cat began to kill the rat;
The rat began to gnaw the rope;
The rope began to hang the butcher;
The butcher began to kill the ox;
The ox began to drink the water;
The water began to quench the fire;
The fire began to burn the stick;
The stick began to beat the dog;
The dog began to bite the pig;
The pig jumped over the stile,
And so the old woman got home that night.

THIS is the key of the kingdom.
    In that kingdom there is a city.
In that city there is a town.
In that town there is a street.
In that street there is a lane.
In that lane there is a yard.
In that yard there is a house.
In that house there is a room.
In that room there is a bed.
On that bed there is a basket.
In that basket there are some flowers.
Flowers in the basket, basket in the bed,
    bed in the room, &c. &c.

RELICS

WILLY boy, Willy boy, where are you going?
I'll go with you, if I may.
"I'm going to the meadow to see them a mowing;
I'm going to help them make hay."

THE girl in the lane, that couldn't speak plain,
  Cried, "Gobble, gobble, gobble."
The man on the hill, that couldn't stand still,
  Went hobble, hobble, hobble.

HINK, minx! the old witch winks,
  The fat begins to fry:
There's nobody at home but little jumping Joan,
  Father, mother, and **I**.

HANNAH BANTRY in the pantry,
  Eating a mutton bone;
How she gnawed it, how she clawed it,
  When she found she was alone!

LITTLE Miss Muffet
  Sat on a tuffet,
Eating of curds and whey;
There came a spider,
And sat down beside her,
And frightened Miss Muffet away.

"What are Little Boys made of?"

WHAT are little boys made of, made of;
    What are little boys made of?
"Snaps and snails, and puppy-dogs' tails;
And that's what little boys are made of, made of."

What are little girls made of, made of, made of;
What are little girls made of?
"Sugar and spice, and all that's nice;
And that's what little girls are made of, made of."

WHAT'S the news of the day,
    Good neighbour, I pray?
"They say the balloon
Is gone up to the moon."

KING'S SUTTON is a pretty town,
    And lies all in a valley;
There is a pretty ring of bells,
    Besides a bowling-alley:
Wine and liquor in good store,
    Pretty maidens plenty;
Can a man desire more?
    There ain't such a town in twenty.

COME, let's to bed,
    Says Sleepy-head;
    "Tarry a while," says Slow;
"Put on the pot,"
Says Greedy-gut,
    "Let's sup before we go."

GIRLS and boys, come out to play;
The moon doth shine as bright as day;
Leave your supper, and leave your sleep,
And come with your playfellows into the street.
Come with a whoop, come with a call,
Come with a good will or not at all.
Up the ladder and down the wall,
A halfpenny roll will serve us all.
You find milk, and I'll find flour,
And we'll have a pudding in half-an-hour.

HOW many days has my baby to play?
　　Saturday, Sunday, Monday,
Tuesday, Wednesday, Thursday, Friday,
Saturday, Sunday, Monday.

AROUND the green gravel the grass grows green,
　　And all the pretty maids are plain to be seen;
Wash them with milk, and clothe them with silk,
And write their names with a pen and ink.

AS I was going to sell my eggs,
　　I met a man with bandy legs,
Bandy legs and crooked toes;
I tripped up his heels, and he fell on his nose.

MY little old man and I fell out;
　　I'll tell you what 'twas all about:
I had money, and he had none,
And that's the way the row begun.

Daffy-
Down-
Dilly
has come
up to
town

In a
yellow
petticoat
and a
green
gown.

DARBY and Joan were dress'd in black,
Sword and buckle behind their back;
Foot for foot, and knee for knee,
Turn about Darby's company.

IF all the seas were one sea,
What a *great* sea that would be!
And if all the trees were one tree,
What a *great* tree that would be!
And if all the axes were one axe,
What a *great* axe that would be!
And if all the men were one man,
What a *great* man he would be!
And if the *great* man took the *great* axe,
And cut down the *great* tree,
And let it fall into the *great* sea,
What a splish splash *that* would be!

RAIN, rain, go away;
Come again another day;
Little Arthur wants to play.

BARBER, barber, shave a pig ;
  How many hairs will make a wig ?
"Four-and-twenty, that's enough : "
Give the barber a pinch of snuff.

LITTLE Tom Tucker
    Sings for his supper;
What shall he eat?
White bread and butter.
How shall he cut it,
Without e'er a knife?
How will he be married
Without e'er a wife?

WHO comes here?
    "A grenadier."
"What do you want?"
    "A pot of beer."
"Where is your money?"
    "I've forgot."
"Get you gone,
    You drunken sot!"

TO market, to market, to buy a plum-cake;
    Back again, back again, baby is late;
To market, to market, to buy a plum-bun,
Back again, back again, market is done.

BLOW, wind, blow! and go, mill, go!
That the miller may grind his corn;
That the baker may take it,
And into rolls make it,
And send us some hot in the morn.

A MAN went a hunting at Reigate,
And wished to leap over a high gate;
Says the owner, "Go round,
With your gun and your hound,
For you never shall leap over my gate."

2 M

THERE was a little nobby colt,
   His name was Nobby Gray;
His head was made of pouce straw,
   His tail was made of hay.
      He could ramble, he could trot,
      He could carry a mustard-pot,
      Round the town of Woodstock,
      Hey, Jenny, hey!

WE'RE all in the dumps,
   For diamonds are trumps;
The kittens are gone to St. Paul's!
   The babies are bit,
   The moon's in a fit,
And the houses are built without walls.

Notes.

THE origin of the right nursery rhymes is, of course, popular, like the origin of ballads, tales (*Märchen*), riddles, proverbs, and, indeed, of literature in general. They are probably, in England, of no great antiquity, except in certain cases, where they supply the words to some child's *ballet*, some dance game. A game may be of prehistoric antiquity, as appears in the rudimentary forms of backgammon, *Pachisi* and *Patullo*, common to Asia, and to the Aztecs, as Dr. Tylor has demonstrated. The child's game—

> "Buck, buck,
> How many fingers do I hold up?"

was known in ancient Rome as *bucca*, though it would be audacious to infer that it survived in Britain since the Norman Conquest. Hop-scotch is also exceedingly ancient, and the curious will find the theories of its origin in Mr. Gomme's learned work on Children's Dances and Songs, published by the Folk-

Lore Society.　Dr. Nicholson's book on the Folk - Lore of Children in Sutherland, still unpublished when I write, may also be consulted.　One of the songs collected by Dr. Nicholson was copied down by a Danish traveller in London during the reign of Charles II.　Robert Chambers's "Popular Rhymes of Scotland" is also a treasure of this kind of antiquities.　It is probable that the Lowland rhymes have occasionally Gaelic counterparts, as the nursery tales certainly have, but I am unacquainted with any researches on this topic by Celtic scholars.

In Mr. Halliwell's Collection, from which this volume is abridged, no manuscript authority goes further back than the reign of Henry VIII., though King Arthur and Robin Hood are mentioned.　The obscure Scottish taunt, levelled at Edward I. when besieging Berwick, is much in the manner of a nursery rhyme :—

> "Kyng Edward,
> 　When thu havest Berwic,
> 　　Pike thee!
> 　When thu havest geton,
> 　　Dike thee!"

This, as Sir Herbert Maxwell says, "seems deficient in salt," but was felt to be irritating by the greatest of the Plantagenets. The jingles on the King of France, against the Scots in the time of James I., against the Tory, or Irish rapparee, and about the Gunpowder Plot, are of the late sixteenth and early seventeenth centuries.　The Great Rebellion supplies "Hector Protector" and "The Parliament soldiers are gone to the king;" "Over the water and over the sea" (or lee) is a parody of a Jacobite ditty of 1748, and refers genially to that love of ale and wine which Prince Charles displayed as early as he showed military courage, at the age of fourteen, when he distinguished himself at the siege of Gaeta. His grandfather, James II., lives in "The rhyme for *porringer ;*" his father in "Jim and George were two great lords." *Tout finit par des chansons.*

Of non-historical jingles, Mr. Halliwell found traces in MSS. as old as the fifteenth century. But it would be a very rare accident that led to their being written down when nobody dreamed of studying Folk-Lore with solemnity. "Thirty days hath September" occurs in the "Return from Parnassus," of Shakspeare's date, and a few snatches, like "When I was a little boy," occur in Shakspeare himself, just as a German version of "My Minnie me slew" comes in Goethe's *Faust.* Indeed, the scraps of magical versified spells in *Märchen* are entirely of the character of nursery rhymes, and are of dateless antiquity. The rhyme of "Dr. Faustus" may be nearly as old as the mediæval legend dramatised by Marlowe. The Elizabethan and Jacobean dramatists put nursery rhymes in the mouths of characters ; a few jingles creep into the Miscellanies, such as "The Pills to purge Melancholy." Among these (1719) is "Tom the piper's son," who played "Over the hills and far away," a song often adapted to Jacobite uses. In 1719, when the Spanish plan of aid to James III. collapsed, pipers must have been melancholy enough.

Melismata (1611) already knows the "Frog who lived in a well," and in *Deuteromelia* (1609) occurs the "Three blind mice." On the Riddles, or *Devinettes*, chapters might be, and have been written. They go back to Samson's time, at least, and are as widely distributed as proverbs, even among Wolufs and Fijians. The most recent discussion is in Mr. Max Müller's "Contributions to the Science of Mythology" (1897). For using "charms," like

"Come, butter, come," many an old woman was burned by the wisdom of our ancestors. Such versified charms, *deducunt carmina lunam*, are the *karakias* of the Maoris, and the *mantras* of Indian superstition. The magical papyri of ancient Egypt are full of them. In our own rhyme, "Hiccup," regarded as a personal kind of fiend ("Animism"), is charmed away by a promise of a butter-cake. There is a collection of such things in Reginald Scot's "Discovery of Witchcraft." Thus our old nursery rhymes are smooth stones from the brook of time, worn round by constant friction of tongues long silent. We cannot hope to make new nursery rhymes, any more than we can write new fairy tales.

Index · of · First · Lines

THE END